A Drop in the Night

The Life and Secret Mission of a World War II Airman

Royce A. Fulmer with
Thea Rademacher

Flint Hills Publishing

A Drop in the Night
The Life and Secret Mission of a World War II Airman
© 2014 Royce A. Fulmer and
Thea Rademacher

Flint Hills Publishing
Topeka, Kansas

www.flinthillspublishing.com

Printed in the U.S.A.
ISBN-10: 150094727X
ISBN-13: 978-1500947279

This book is dedicated to my pilot William L. Borden and the rest of my crew: co-pilot Vernon Doran, Navigator Jack Barton, Bombardier James Bruning, Gunner Harry Kieschnick, Radio Operator Max Dinsmore, and Gunner Stacy Phillips.

Royce A. Fulmer

TABLE OF CONTENTS

PROLOGUE
That's What Neighbors Do

The progressive dinner of a few neighbors promised nothing unusual. I looked forward to good food, wine, and conversation with people I wanted to get to know better. Our neighborhood is the kind that offers the privilege of space. We measure our yards not in feet but acres, three is the average. The distance between our homes seemed to discourage connections. Time for cultivating new friendships was limited; my husband and I had our hands full with two young sons and a third on the way. As neighbors, we gave friendly waves and bought fund-raising cookies and popcorn from each other's children, but our knowledge focused primarily on exterior views of

1

how we lived. We had not taken the time to share our stories. I hoped our dinner together would change that.

At the last stop of our dinner party, I was seated to the left of a handsome man in his early 70s. He was known throughout our area for the commercial development projects he spearheaded and construction of upscale homes. His recently completed home, adjacent to my own, had been one of his projects. When we built our home a few years prior, our view to the north was a mostly-dry creek bed outlined by old cottonwood trees. To the south was a field full of native wildflowers. I had mixed feelings when I saw the field being broken by a dirty bulldozer for the foundation of the home that would be built next door. It would become a two-story house with a circle driveway in the front. A tall flagpole was planted firmly next to the middle of the arched driveway. Before the house was completed, soil was turned for a large garden for vegetables. Native limestone rocks weighing tons were placed around a fire pit.

The man who moved into this house with his wife and two children intrigued me. He left for work at the crack of dawn. He came home in the evening and quickly began work again, this time in his yard. He seemed as energetic as his two teenage children, but his white hair and wrinkles around his eyes reminded me of grandpas and great uncles from my youth. His wife, who loved to play tennis and had the figure to prove it, shared his devotion to taking care of their yard. She drove their riding lawn mower like she was racing to be first at the finish line. I couldn't help but notice how much time they spent together; and the difference in their ages, 27 years, made them a couple like none I had known before.

The first time I spoke with my neighbor, I said, "I'm going to have a baby!" I was eight months pregnant. Standing just a few feet away from me, I could see that the man had intelligent brown eyes that reminded me of my papa. He replied with a friendly laugh, "Well, you are, are you?"

Later that summer the man walked over to talk with me when he saw me staring intently at the ground in my back yard. Living outside the city limits meant we were on our own with our home waste disposal. My septic system was not working. I had "septic tank failure." There was wastewater bubbling up in my back yard about 30 feet from my house. "Oh shit," the man said. "What we've got to do here," he continued, taking instant command of the problem, "we've got to get this system inspected, see what we're dealin' with. I'll get my guy on it." He kept his word and in record time I was told by the man, "What we're gonna' do is put in a trans-flow evaporation bed. We'll cut off the lines to the basement, keep that system goin', it'll just put less pressure on it. We'll use the evaporation bed for the rest of the house." He assured me this was "no real big deal" and that it would be much less expensive than constructing an entirely new septic system for my house. I asked him how much I would owe him for his share of the work. "Well, nothing," he replied with absolute sincerity. I felt overwhelmed by his generosity. When I asked him why he was doing this for me and my family he stated matter-of-factly, "Because that's what neighbors do."

I knew what my neighbor had done for me and I knew how hard he worked. I also knew he would take time to relax. Like many in my family who worked the land as farmers, this man would sit in a folding aluminum lawn chair at dusk, dog by his side, and watch the cloud formations change and cars drive by.

But I didn't really know anything of substance about his past. Eating a meal together seemed like a good way to get to know him better.

At the final leg of our dinner party, the man's wife was to his right. Next to her was a red-headed journalist who walked her matching golden retriever past my house twice a day. I had become friendly with the woman and learned that she was the editor-in-chief of a respected magazine funded by our state. Just as I had hoped, the tradition of sharing stories around Kansas dinner tables happened that night. We began our evening with appetizers at the home at the top of the street. Our hosts were a long-married couple who had raised two daughters and shared a compassion to help, he as a psychologist, she as a social worker. Salad was served at the home of the red-haired journalist and her husband. They both had demanding jobs; he was a litigation attorney. Like my neighbors, their yard was an important part of their lives, sharing homemade pies made from cherry trees lining their driveway and encouraging my family to use their pool anytime we wanted.

The main meal took place at my neighbor's home. It was the first time I had been inside the house. I was struck with how cozy the house felt despite its large size. Not since being in my own grandma's house had I been in a home so perfectly clean. It smelled of coffee-scented candles and was full of interesting books.

Dessert took place at my house. My mother, a woman with deep roots to the farmlands of Kansas, had splurged and bought an expensive orange liqueur for us to share. Our stomachs were stretched from food and sore from laughing. By dessert, we felt comfortable being together. The man started talking about flying in World War II. His wife interjected, "He never talked about his past, but now he can't stop!" I asked him what kind of airplane he flew and where. "I made a few flights into France to make some deliveries." "What kind of deliveries?" my mother asked. The journalist and I leaned in to hear his answer. "Mostly people," he replied. "Sometimes they tried to change their minds at the last moment, but then we just kinda' gave them a nudge outa' the airplane." We sat in silence for a moment. Finally, I spoke, "And?"

CHAPTER 1
Necessity Invents a Top-Secret Mission

Forty-two years after the end of World War II, one of the best kept secrets of the war was finally revealed. From the fall of 1943 until the spring of 1945, over three thousand American soldiers were involved in a special operation so secret that most of them were not aware of the scope of the campaign or even the name of the mission. Code named "Operation Carpetbagger," the mission put these young men in highly unusual circumstances. Trained as bomber crews, the Carpetbaggers didn't drop bombs; their skills were used for other purposes. Their special cargo included radio sets, weapons designed for sabotage, and even pigeons trained to carry secret messages to London. They also carried spies, both men and women, who had volunteered to be parachuted deep into Nazi-occupied areas.

On May 10, 1940, Nazi Germany unleashed a *Blitzkrieg* on France. This new approach to warfare was not like former wars where battles would develop slowly and be dominated by infantry and artillery. Rather, the German Army attacked with unprecedented speed. They struck at France through the invasion of Belgium and the Netherlands. France would fall to the Nazis with a death toll of 100,000 and 200,000 wounded. The French Army had been crushed. Denmark, Belgium, the Netherlands, and Luxembourg had fallen into German hands.

The people of France were in a state of shock after their government's surrender. The magnitude of the German *Blitzkrieg* stunned many as they had been reassured that France could withstand a German attack. Despite their aggressive strategies, the Germans had encountered resistance and causalities of 27,000. A young French officer, Charles de Gaulle, was able to flee to London. In a speech broadcast to his countrymen he proclaimed, "Whatever happens, the flame of French resistance must not and will not be extinguished."

Germany's stunning successes tipped the balance of power in Europe. In less than a year, Hitler had conquered most of the continent. Great Britain had not provided an effective defense against Germany during the invasion of France. At the time, Winston Churchill who had just become Prime Minister on May 10, 1940, reasoned that British efforts in the struggle against this invasion on the Continent would be ineffective. The success of the Nazis in France made it clear to Churchill that Britain was at risk and needed to prepare a defense. The United States still remained neutral though President Franklin D. Roosevelt had begun to take action unilaterally to send weapons and warplanes to Great Britain. For the next four years after Germany's invasion of France, Great Britain fought a war by air and sea away from the Western Front. Not until D-Day, June 1944, did a major British Army return to France.

In spite of Nazi occupation, a resistance movement began to emerge in France and surrounding countries. These determined fighters were small groups of armed men and women who came from all economic, religious, and cultural backgrounds of society. Liberals, anarchists, communists, Roman Catholics—including priests—and Jews participated in dangerous covert operations against the Nazis and Vichy government, France's fascist puppet state. The tasks the Resistance members performed were as varied as their backgrounds. Underground newspapers were written and distributed. Critical intelligence was gathered and smuggled to the Allies. Soldiers and downed Airmen who found themselves in enemy territory were rescued and sent home by a system of escape networks.

The Gestapo reacted quickly to these new forces and attempted to hunt them down. Many Resistance members retreated to the forests to hide. One of the most famous groups, "The Marquis," took their name from a type of scrub bush found in the high ground of Southeastern France. Initially, the Resistance forces were disorganized, but as German occupation into their country grew, so did the sophistication of the resistance. By November of 1942, German forces occupied all of France. Compulsory labor service was required by the Germans and the persecution of Jews continued to grow. Two years later the Resistance Movement in France alone numbered over 100,000 members. The growth of the Resistance had been aided by a clandestine operation with Great Britain. Beginning in May of 1941, the first British secret agent of the Special Operations Executive, or SOE, was dropped into northern France. Britain and the Resistance fighters were beginning a vital relationship. Britain supplied the French with trained agents, arms, and equipment; the French in return supplied vital intelligence reports.

By the spring of 1944, sixty intelligence cells had the sole mission of gathering specific intelligence that would lead up to D-Day. In May of 1944 alone, over 3,000 written reports and 700 wireless reports were smuggled to the Allies. Well-placed explosives destroyed over 1,800 railway engines. Infrastructure critical to the Nazis movement of equipment and lines of communication and lines of supply were destroyed by the Resistance. General Dwight D. Eisenhower, aware of the skills of the Resistance fighters, requested the BBC send coded messages asking for actions to support the D-Day landings. The purpose was to cause distractions and disruptions to help the Allied forces establish a beachhead on the Normandy Coast and to hinder the German response. These actions were effective. Armed groups were able to slow the arrival of the German Second SS Panzer Division at Normandy.

The Resistance efforts did not go unnoticed by the Nazis. In an act of brutal retaliation, a group of German soldiers led by Major Otto Kickmann raided the French village of Oradour-sur-Glane, executing over 600 men, women, and children before burning the village to the ground. The German policy of reprisal against French civilians for the acts of Resistance fighters was nothing new. The Nazis had a policy of reprisal against civilians living in any town or village close to where covert actions were carried out.

The sacrifices made by the French Resistance and the people of France were great. Their significant accomplishments were noted by Supreme Allied Commander Eisenhower when he wrote in his memoirs, "Throughout France the Resistance had been of inestimable value in the campaign. Without their great assistance, the liberation of France would have consumed a much longer time and meant greater losses to ourselves." The French Resistance's role as a force against the Nazis has been long known and recognized.

However, the role of a relatively small handful of American Airmen is less known but nonetheless important. In the fall of 1943, the newly-formed top-secret arm of the United States responsible for coordinating secret espionage, the Office of Strategic Services, or OSS, had begun to work on a collaborative project with Britain's SOE. Operation Carpetbagger, a top-secret mission to aid Resistance forces fighting Nazi occupation, was about to begin. This is the story of one of those formerly unknown heroes, a rough country boy who just wanted to fly.

CHAPTER 2
"While I breathe, I hope."

South Carolina State Motto

By the time Royce Alton Fulmer enlisted in the United States Army Air Corps on October 10, 1942, his life experiences had already made him tougher than hell. Growing up in rural South Carolina in the 1920s and '30s, this little boy, now a young man, faced extremely challenging circumstances. His decision to enlist was prompted by a number of things: he needed to get away from the wrong crowd, he felt a sense of duty to support his country, he longed to escape poverty, the law was breathing down his neck. But mostly, he wanted to learn all he could about airplanes.

Royce Fulmer was born in Winnsboro, South Carolina just a little over six decades after South Carolina Unionist James L. Petigru declared his state's decision to secede, "unwise as it is too small to be a nation and too large to be an insane asylum." Rural South Carolina in the 1920s had not recovered from the ravages of the Civil War. Royce began his life in a house on a plantation whose owners once had slaves. The home now belonged to Royce's maternal aunt, Belle Martin Reeder. She had moved there with her first husband. Though the slave houses as well as the husband were gone, the road marking where slaves lived was still there. Royce recalls, *"The house was a big son-of-a-bitch. It didn't have columns. It wasn't that style. The first floor was five feet off the ground, sittin' on a brick foundation. There were big steps leading to the house, probably twenty feet wide."* This home where Aunt Belle lived was full of children, up to sixteen at one time. It was also full of history. General Sherman used the house as a headquarters when he burned a swath sixty miles through the countryside to nearby Columbia where the secession movement began. *"The scars are still on the state house where Sherman shelled it. They've got metal stars on the state house now where the shells hit and chipped off pieces."*

Royce's mother, Lessie Mae Martin, was born in the last year of the nineteenth century. *"She was a loving person, a good-looking woman. She was too pretty to work in the field so Aunt Belle was the one who worked in the field. Mom could be smart, but she could be dumber than shit with men."* Lessie Mae's decision to marry Robert Birts Fulmer when she was 20 years old resulted in three children: a boy, James Madison, born in 1917; a girl, Helen Keith, born in 1920; and Royce three years later. Robert's World War I draft registration card lists him as "short, medium build, blue eyes, light hair, not bald, not disabled." The 1920 U.S. Census reports that he rented his home, could read and write, and made his living as a farmer. This is more information than Royce ever knew. *"The only time I can remember him, I must have been about six or seven. I was living with my Granddaddy Martin then. He came by to see me, I guess. And of course I didn't have any shoes at this point. He drew an outline of my foot out on a newspaper. Gonna send me some shoes. I never did hear anything from him. Never heard from him again."*

Without a husband to help house and feed her three small children, Lessie Mae made the decision to divide the siblings. Royce's oldest brother went to live with the mother of the father Royce never knew. *"Grandma Fulmer had a farm. Grandma, she had some bucks and she wanted to take the oldest boy. He went to live with her and she raised him. He was her boy. She gave him money all the time. He was spoiled rotten. He was takin' advantage of her all the time."*

Royce, his mother, and his older sister went to live in the big house with Aunt Belle and her collection of children. He started school while living there with his siblings and cousins. Aunt Belle and his mother saw that Royce began the first grade at Chalkhill Elementary. *"There was an open mine where they had chalk veins. Back in those days we didn't have chalk for the blackboard. We would just pick it up in chunks. Had three or four different colors: white, blue, and red. You'd pick out your piece and shape it, carve it to make it pointed. I don't remember what the school was like. I wasn't interested in it. I was interested in making money."*

In the decade leading up to the Great Depression, South Carolina's agriculturally-based economy was already suffering. The conclusion of World War I had also brought with it an end for what had been a significant demand for products grown in the state. Now farmers found their methods stripped the soil of its productivity. Years of cotton production had depleted the soil and an infestation of boll weevils from Mexico damaged the crops that remained. Farmers had borrowed too much money and half the banks in the state had failed. Property values tanked. *"I can't tell you into words how poor we were. We didn't have shoes for years. We didn't always have enough food. We grew sweet potatoes and ate them with milk. We made our own bread. We ate milk and bread or milk and cornbread for dinner. We raised meat, cured it. And we ate wild animals."*

Not only were wild animals a regular part of the family diet, Royce and his older sister thought they might make good pets. *"My sister and I, when I was about six or seven, had seen a squirrel in a cage. We decided we wanted one for a pet. We looked for a hollow tree with a hole in it. It would be slick at the entrance to the hole, worn from them going in and out. I was pretty good with an axe and I cut a hole in that hollow tree. The tail was hanging out—we could see it. I must have missed hitting the squirrel by five inches. We were excited! I grabbed him by the tail and pulled him out, had my hands run up his back, trying to get behind the head. I got to the shoulders and he flipped around and bit my knuckle! He wouldn't turn loose so my sister, nine or ten years old, had to kill him while that squirrel's teeth were stuck in my hand. She got a stick or a rock to do the job. There was some blood, yes. She killed the squirrel and had to pry him off even after he was dead. He didn't want to turn loose. We took him home and ate him. My hand swelled up to double in size."*

Doctors may have been making house calls at that time in other parts of the country, but in rural South Carolina when the captured squirrel refused to let go of Royce, no doctors came around his neighborhood. *"The adults thought we had been kind'a stupid. But we ran around on our own all the time. We climbed trees, hunted for animals. To prepare a squirrel to eat, you cut the squirrel up and you got legs with a joint in it, four of those, eight pieces of leg, two pieces of back. That was what I liked. Had some breast part of it. Of course you cut the head off. We ate squirrel a couple times a week, just one at a meal. I don't remember what it tasted like. It was fried in lard. Ever damn thing was fried in lard and you just salt and peppered it."*

Even though he was young, Royce understood how basic his family's existence was. At an age when children are just starting school, Royce wanted to make money. He learned to operate a plow pulled by a mule when he was eight. Lack of nutrition slowed his growth but not his determination to maneuver a plow around the corners of a field. Before he was a teenager, Royce picked cotton on his knees, doubling his production by using both hands to reach into the sharp boll that held the cotton. *"Hell no, there were no gloves."* He operated a grisly machine called a "stalk cutter" that over 80 years later still makes him shake his head in disbelief that a boy was allowed to do what should have only been a man's work. *"A stalk cutter was the most dangerous son-of-a-bitch. It had a platform with a big wheel underneath with blades on it. It would run along, push the stock down and chop it up. It was a two-mule deal. One time I was on that thing and I ran into a tree stump. Stopped the whole damned thing. I fell down between the mules. Got out of that deal. The mules were a little excited, crazy sons-a-bitches. I must have been six-years-old. Would work that thing in the field by myself."*

Another tool was too large for young hands, but still Royce worked alongside the men. *"You know what a scythe is? Got a sharp, curved blade hooked on the end of a handle. On the back of the blade is a wooden cradle that the wheat falls into. You sweep it around and drop the stalk on the ground."* This primitive tool was over five feet long, so a young Royce's job was to walk behind the men gathering the fallen crop. With a cradle attached to the scythe, the grain would fall in one direction making it relatively easier to bundle. *"Then you come up and tie that by hand for wheat or rye. You use a stalk itself as a tie. The bundles, about ten inches wide, would be run through the thrashing machine."* Swinging the scythes slowly across the field, the field workers' rhythm was broken only by the necessity every few rows of re-sharpening dulled blades. The men who cut and gathered the wheat had been hired by Royce's grandfather. This backbreaking work provided a temporary distraction from the poverty faced beyond the days of harvest.

Royce was always thinking about ways to earn money. *"That was my money maker; the rabbit boxes. I made rabbit boxes out of scrap wood or hollo' trees. Had about ten of those boxes. Sold a rabbit for a quarter each. Sold them live. The rabbit would come in the box, trip the back lever, then the door would come down. Rabbits play on sandbars. I would see their tracks and put the boxes there. I caught wild rabbit, big ol' fat wild rabbits. I had a small pony, 'Pick.' I'd ride him with a rabbit under each arm. I'd put the rabbit's feet between my fingers and then had to jump on that pony holding onto those rabbits. Sometimes the rabbit would scratch the pony and try to throw your ass off, but I wouldn't let those rabbits get away. I needed to sell them for money. I kept them in a cage before I sold them. No, I didn't keep the money for myself."*

Though he often did the work of grown men, Royce was still a child who had an instinct for play. He enjoyed making his own toys. While looking at a wooden toy he whittled over 80 years ago, he recalls, *"What you do is put a string through the hole in the neck. Tap on it and it dances; both feet and arms swing and everthin'."* Royce laughed at the realization that the toy, "Jackie Limber Legs," had the shoes he didn't. *"How I did all that,* (the U-shaped space connecting the moveable pieces) *I had nothing to cut that out; had to do it with my knife blade. No tools. Has a cap built on there, see?"* This wasn't Royce's only self-made entertainment. *"Same time I was making this I was screwin' up the wall in the kitchen of Granddaddy Martin's house. There was a wooden wall with tongue and groove siding, no paint. On that wall I had my machine running. The women did a lot of sewing. I got a lot of spools from people. I put a lot of spools on that wall and some of them I had rubber bands on and the others I just had a string on. I'd have four or five of those, pulling on those, working on those belts. Pulley and belts."*

At times, Royce's playground was dangerous. An attempt to make a banjo when he was eight or nine resulted in a scar on his left hand that is still visible. *"I had found a round cake pan. Had a piece of wood and I made me a neck. I was hewing that neck out* with a sharp axe. I was holding it up, chippin' that wood with the axe. I hit my hand with the axe and ripped that whole thing right off (the fleshy part of his palm). Scar's still there."

Royce and his cousin Zuleime, he called her "Zu," loved to play alone in the woods. "*We would be gone all day. We would eat anything in season, halls, persimmons. We called 'em halls, a little berry about the size of your finger, turn yellow, had a seed. Anyway, we'd eat some of those persimmons and we had pecans. Crack 'em with my teeth. We'd climb the damn trees. A neighbor had a mean bull in the pasture by Aunt Belle's. He'd come after ya. We'd climb this tall persimmon tree. Must have been thirty minutes to an hour with that son-of-a-bitch bull pawing and being mean. He finally left and we could come down.*"

Cows could pose a problem as well for fearless children. "*We were watching the cow graze. I was around cows a lot; I milked them every morning before school. For some reason, this ol' milk cow had horns that turned in. Some way or other my suspenders on my overalls got caught on her horn. I was petting her, and she got excited and started turning around fast like a merry-go-round and hooked my suspenders in the back. Zu had to run to the house to get Aunt Belle. I broke loose before that. It was just one of those things that happen to ya, you know."*

Supernatural stories originating from local legends fueled the imagination of a young Royce. *"My Granddaddy Martin, he had a horse and buggy he drove all the time. We would ride in that buggy to go to church. My mother is buried at the cemetery by that Baptist church. It was a country road, more of a one-lane path, really. There was a section of that path, there was something there. A light would get up by your horses' bridle and somethin' would walk you through there. I'm sure there was something there. You would feel a difference."*

Death was often on the minds of the working poor in rural South Carolina. The weakness of the state's economy crippled South Carolina's health care. The state treasury could not support the few services it had provided in the past. In 1933, the Bureau of State Hygiene ceased to function when Federal money was withdrawn and the state had no money to replace those funds. That same year, the state's empty coffers led to the elimination of the job of state epidemiologist. Without a health system in place, or vaccines like tetanus, a scrape against rusty metal could severely damage unprotected skin. "*My sister Keith and I, a neighbor gave us a little hound puppy, a brown lab. We brought him home with a string around his neck, about a mile or two. Anyway, he grew up to be a pretty good pet. I was visiting one time at Aunt Belle's and I jumped over the pasture gate. It had a nail sticking up, and I just gouged out a place on my right calf.*" Royce shows the inch-and-a-half scar on his leg to help illustrate the point. "*My leg was all swelled up, and of course we didn't have a doctor or anything. This damned dog would just lick it. Every night for a couple a' weeks he would lick that son-of-a-bitch and clean it up until it healed up. You know what 'proud flesh' is? It's decaying flesh, yellow color. My leg got proud flesh cause I didn't put anything on it. Well certainly it needed stiches. It really didn't hurt a lot. The dog would clean it up, and finally that damned thing healed up.*"

An infected leg may have seemed trivial to Royce given other things he saw as a child involving death. "*I must have been six, just starting school, when I found this guy dead. He lived in a house with his brother. They were bachelors and had eight or ten hound dogs. Doc and Oliver Backman were the two guys' names. They lived about two miles away, across a pond and through the woods. For some reason Doc came over to visit and I was told to go check on Oliver and he was dead. I tried to wake him up but he was stiff. His eyes were open. I come running back of course to tell 'em. They burried him in the family graveyard. I watched 'em make a box for him out of used lumber, two-by-eight box. They lined the inside of it with black crepe paper. I watched 'em put his body in the box and they nailed the top shut."*

Fatherless until he was four, Lessie Mae met another man who would become Royce's stepfather. His mother married George Tillman Williams, "Tillman" as Royce refers to him. There were three more children from this marriage: Savonne, Hayne, and Tillman Jr. Lessie Mae's marriage to Tillman meant Royce left his beloved Aunt Belle's house for a place further out in the country. The new and growing family would move around a lot. Their first home was on a large cotton farm owned by Tillman's father. Step-grandpa Williams had been born in January of

1863; the Civil War would not end for over two years. Royce's new step-grandfather lived in a *"nice, big house. There was a big barn with several horses there and mules for pullin' the plows."*

Royce and his family owned little more than their time. When he did work, Tillman scratched out his living as a sharecropper. These farmers without land rented tired soil and hoped for decent weather. They often found themselves in debt to owners who wrote the law. Living conditions reflected their poverty; homes rented by the Fulmer/Tillman family always lacked water, electricity, and plaster.

Royce, who was still in grade school when his mother remarried, did not have a positive first impression of Tillman. *"He was a spoiled brat. His daddy got him out of jail because he killed a guy. Tillman's daddy was a big cotton farmer. Got his son a shorter sentence. Also supported him at times."* Royce saw an opportunity to earn some money himself. Along with the grown men his step-grandfather employed to work in the fields, Royce plowed behind a mule and helped plant cotton, earning twenty-five cents a day.

Royce recalls he and his stepfather got along *"pretty good."* He remembers fishing in a creek with him that was full of eels. *"They don't have any feet. They look about like a snake. Their mouth is a little bit different. You couldn't tell the difference hardly if you skin them out. The place where we fished must have been about fifteen to twenty feet wide, trees overhung both sides. It was pretty deep. You could pull yourself along in the boat by the limbs. Once in a while a snake would fall off the limbs into the boat. Hell yes, we ate eels."*

Tillman was a violent man who exposed his family to dangerous criminals. The third of four moves in as many years found the family deep in South Carolina back country. The closest town to this hardscrabble land was Swansea. The third house Tillman took Royce to sat on wooden blocks a couple feet off the ground. The main part of the house consisted of a living room, bedrooms, and a shed off to the side. There was a door in the back opening to a walkway leading to another building. This structure contained a fireplace and served as the cooking and eating area. There were no glass windows, only shutters that just marginally kept out the rain and the rare snow.

Unwanted elements came in more forms to this house. Royce's stepfather, who was no stranger to criminal activity himself, had met a man named Fred Williams Poole when they were both children. Royce's stepfather witnessed "Pop Poole's" first criminal act when, as a young boy, he stole a hat. Future illegal acts would become more serious, eventually landing Poole on the FBI's Most Wanted List in 1944.

"Poole and his partner stopped at our house in the country. They were splittin' up the loot. They had robbed a service station. They had a suitcase open full of cash and things they'd robbed. I was playing under the house because it was dry, and I could listen to them through a crack in the floor. The men must a' heard me because they came out of the bedroom. Poole gave me my first scout knife. It had a corkscrew and a couple of blades. I must have been probably six years old, maybe five."

Poole saw an opportunity to use the inquisitive little boy he found playing under the house. Poole asked Royce to come into town with him to get some bread. Royce was impressed by Poole's car, a new yellow 1929 Buick Coupe. Looking back on it now, Royce realizes that Poole was using him as a screen to divert attention. Royce never asked why "Public Enemy Number One" was walking around Swansea, South Carolina buying bread with a little boy. In Royce's young mind that had known nothing but poverty, he thought Poole's lifestyle was enticing. "*I thought it was a hell-of-a-deal. He had money, a car. He treated me nice. Took me to the store and was nice to me.*"

The FBI had a different impression of Poole. During one of Poole's visits, a team of men from the Bureau raided Royce's house. "*The FBI burst into the house with submachine guns. There were two or three agents. One picked up a big pistol that was on the fireplace mantel in the front living room. The agents ran through the house, down the walkway to the kitchen. Poole was sitting at the table there; my mother had been cooking him some breakfast. He heard them comin' and jumped out the window. There was no glass. The agents ran to that window and started shooting their machine guns. Poole ran underneath the grape arbor that was about 20 feet from the window and followed the path to the outhouse. They shot that outhouse to pieces. Poole* had his new Buick parked down in the woods behind the outhouse and escaped in his car."

Frustrated by their failure to catch Poole, Royce recalls an agent asking for his stepfather's help in setting up a trap to catch Poole. *"The FBI wanted Stepdaddy to call Fred back in so they could shoot him. My stepdad said he wouldn't do that to a friend. We lived across the road from a highway clay pit. Dirt was taken from there to fill in roads. Later on that afternoon, my stepdaddy sent me down the road. He had told me to whistle three times. I did and Fred came out of the woods. He came back to the house with me and Stepdaddy told him what the FBI had said. I'm certain the FBI kept a look out on the house. Things were so different in those days. I don't think Stepdaddy saw him after that. Fred was caught, maybe years later, and put in the pen."*

Tillman may not have seen Fred W. Poole after that, but a thirteen-year-old Royce is sure he did. *"Granddaddy, my mom's dad, played for dances. Mother's brother played the banjo and there were parties at night. The furniture was moved out of the way for room to dance. One night, I'll never forget it, Fred Poole, 'Public Enemy Number One,' was there at a dance. He was sitting on a trunk. I went up to him and asked him if he was Fred Poole. He looked at me and kind of smiled and said, 'No Sonny, I'm not Fred Poole,' but he was on the lam from the cops."* Royce felt he had the evidence to believe this was indeed Poole. During one of his times in prison, Poole made rings from buffalo nickels. The man at the party wore a ring made from a buffalo nickel.

On May 25, 1944, the Federal Bureau of Investigation, United States Department of Justice, issued Identification Order Number 1939 indicating that Fred Williams Poole was wanted for "Unlawful Flight to Avoid Prosecution (Murder)." Identified as 5 foot 7 and a half, 145 pounds with blue eyes and brown hair, the Order cautioned that, "Poole has an extensive criminal record, having been arrested numerous times since 1912 in South Carolina, Maryland, Ohio, and Texas. His criminal specialty is burglary. POOLE HAS TWO MACHINE GUNS AND A .45 AUTOMATIC PISTOL. HE IS DANGEROUS."

During this time in our history, many infamous criminals topped the FBI Most Wanted List. The records of lesser known, but still extremely dangerous ones like Poole, are incomplete. To the best of Royce's knowledge, Poole was caught and sent to prison, killing again, this time a fellow inmate. Royce believes Poole died in prison.

Life with Tillman Williams exposed the family to violence in more ways than just Fred Poole. Tillman was a violent man who physically abused Royce's mother, often in front of the children. *"He would beat her. My sister Keith would jump on him and try to beat him. Keith was a hellcat. She'd fight my stepdad to protect my mom. One time I ran over to Granddaddy Martin's house five miles away or more. Granddaddy came back in a wagon with me and my cousin. He loaded my mom and the rest of the kids in the wagon and took us back to his house. Mom finally left this guy. I'm not sure that he didn't die."* This did happen not too long after Royce's mother left. Tillman died in 1936 at the age of 46.

Poverty kept Royce's family without a stable, consistent home. *"We were passed around. We needed money to make a living. We tried to survive."* After her decision to leave Tillman, Royce's mother and children found refuge at Lessie Mae's childhood home. Royce's maternal grandmother, Mamie Elizabeth Sharp, had died when his mother was seven years old, leaving Grandpa Martin with four young daughters. Grandpa Martin remarried a woman named Annie. They had seven children of their own, one who died in infancy. So, when Royce and his fatherless family arrived, the Martin home was already full of extended family and their children. Still, Royce found love, security, and plenty of opportunities for work at the Martin home. It was here Royce learned a skill that would make him a lot of cash as an older teenager.

"My Granddaddy Martin had a syrup business where he would make syrup, mostly from sugarcane, for other folks. Syrup was a very popular deal on the plate, you know. You could sell it or a guy could pay you to make it. People would bring in their sugarcane and we would put it in separate piles. We'd feed the cane through two big rollers that would squeeze the juice out into a bucket. It took a mule and a couple of guys operating it—big rollers— big steel roller going around, having a mule pull that, like a training ring. We'd take the juices and put it in a flat pan set up on a fire. There are partitions in the syrup pan, a four by twenty-foot pan. And you would have different people's syrups in different partitions

in the pan. We would cook it to the consistency the owner wanted: thinner or thicker."

Syrup wasn't the only popular product created by this process. *"We'd get the fire going under the syrup pan and skimmings would start to form on the top. When you cook syrup, you get all these juices. We had big skimmers that look like they have nail holes in 'em. You just skin that foam off all the time and dump it in this barrel. After the syrup season was done, about September, we'd let the barrel set there until it finished fermenting, a couple a' weeks. We would remove the syrup pan from the fire box and set a little copper still on it. It was a unique still; a homemade deal about four-by-four with a copper cap. That's 'skimmin' liquor' we call it. Granddaddy would use it in warm water, sugar, or somethin' like that. A toddy."*

But like so many other times in Royce's young life, his circumstances would soon change. *"Granddaddy Martin really took care of me. He called me 'Aus' after the little car, the Austin Healy, because I was so small. It was a nickname because I was so under-nursed. Granddaddy was dying in bed. A bunch of people were in the room with him. He called me in and said, 'Aus, I just want you to know that you are just as welcome here as any of these kids here. He told me that."*

At the time of Granddaddy Martin's death, Royce's mother wasn't living with the family. Martin had decided that Royce and the other children needed the security and peace his home could provide and he was determined to give it to them. Despite his deathbed assurance that Royce would always be welcome at his house, Royce was nervous about his situation after Martin's death. His step-grandmother, Annie, found herself with no husband and a house full of children. Royce was determined to prove his usefulness to the household, *"I worked my ass off for her. Worked the garden on Saturdays, cooked breakfast for the family every morning. I was surprised she wouldn't keep me just for the food."*

Royce's premonition that change was coming proved correct. Not too long after his grandfather's death, Royce's mother came to the house with a new boyfriend she had met in Columbia. No effort was made to keep Royce from hearing their conversation. *"Annie told my mother, 'We've got to do something with Royce. We can't feed him anymore.' My mother came to pick me up with a sack of clothes. She and her boyfriend had an old car. She said we were going to Columbia. There was a service station at a fork in the road on the way and we stopped, and my mother bought me a Coke. It just so happened my Aunt Belle was there. She still lived in the big house, about a mile and a half from the service station. She said, 'Oh Royce, you look real nice. How are you doing?' "*

Aunt Belle turned to Royce's mother and asked, *"What are you doing with Royce?"*

Royce's mother responded, *"Miss Annie couldn't feed him anymore, so she wanted me to find a place for him. I don't have anything else to do so I am taking him to the orphanage in Columbia."*

Aunt Belle refused to let her eleven-year-old nephew be sent to an orphanage. *"Oh no, no, no. I got a place for one more at my house."*

This conversation occurred right in front of Royce. *"I was thrilled to death to be going with Aunt Belle to the big house. I had lived there when I was little, vacationed there, and had gotten clothes from them. She took me in down there and I helped her farm. She put me back in school. She talked to the teacher and said I was going to repeat the sixth grade because I wasn't ready for high school. I didn't know my ass from a shotgun 'cause I didn't go to school that much. It was just a dinky-ass school. So, they decided I should go one more year back in the sixth grade to get ready for high school. Best move they made. Mom was thrilled to death that Aunt Belle said she would take me. There were already lots of folks at Aunt Belle's, a brother-in-law and his two kids, her kids, her stepkids, at least. I never blamed my mother for what she did. I knew what the situation was. Can you imagine not being able to feed your kid if he was hungry? When I thought about going to the orphanage, I knew she didn't have any other choice. I didn't think about Aunt Belle. It just happened that she was there in the service station. If I'd a' gone to the orphanage I probably would a' been dead or in jail. I don't know."*

When Royce returned to Aunt Belle's house, she had a new husband, John Dewey Reeder. He would prove to be instrumental in introducing a variety of things to Royce that would shape the direction of his life. Royce describes Reeder as a *"moonshiner, a bootlegger. He would try anything to make money to feed his family."* Royce had always shared the same devotion to his family. Now he had a father figure who would teach him how to make money, regardless of the risks involved.

CHAPTER 3
Runnin' Whiskey

On the cusp of his teen years, Royce forged a relationship with a man who would risk his freedom to support his new family. Royce learned a lot from John Dewey. *"Old man Reeder was against carrying a gun or messin' with young girls. Uncle said, 'don't do that, if you do, don't even call me.' He knew his way around. Hell yes, it was good advice and I took it. I was very good about that. Yeah, I've been smart about that."* Uncle Reeder had additional knowledge he would share with Royce as well.

"It's pretty simple to make a still, really it is. There are all kinds of ways to boil it. You can do it with steam, coke, wood. Start with a beer type deal:

sugar, meal, yeast to make it ferment. Then you add a couple inches of bran, wheat bran, or something like that, and it floats on the top. Then you put some kind a' lid on it. Let it ferment for a week to ten days. When you check it, it should be warm to your touch. It will get hot enough so it's ready to boil then it'll bust the lid off from the boil. When it settles down, put it in the still and boil the alcohol off. Then you put the whole thing into a doubler, boil the whole thing again. The doubler runs off steam; start this with a little mash. Now the whole thing boils again, and you get a higher proof of alcohol. A spout would come out of the condenser. There's a pipe coming into the boiler, inch, half inch off the floor. The alcohol boils off first, then into the condenser that's around a pipe into a creek or something. We liked to do it that way; run pipe down the crick into a bucket to catch it and it would be pure alcohol almost. You can use anything you want to as far as a container. We used fruit jars. I didn't drink it as a habit. Just sip it, taste it, ya know. Very simple operation."

Though simple, the moonshining production and distribution business was not legal. Prohibition had ended in December of 1933; that was no longer the problem. The trouble came from the stills in the swamps. Since the 1890s, South Carolina practiced a "dispensary system" regarding the sale of alcohol; every drop was to be sold in a state-owned liquor store. Getting the illegal "White Lightning" from still to customer required covert delivery. Royce was now a teenager with an eye for cars, a taste for speed, and an uncle who was happy to have Royce involved in the family business.

In his early teens, Royce began going on runs with Uncle Reeder. Most of them took place in the dark of night. *"Stillmore, Georgia. That was a long run. We'd drive all night, not sleep. There was a Greek restaurant down below the train station in Columbia. The old man, he liked aged steak. Have you ever seen aged steak with the green shit on it? Yeah, it was green mold on the steak. That's the only place in town he could get that. I'd eat somethin' else. We'd have a nice dinner about three o'clock in the morning."*

Uncle Reeder did have some strategies he could use to transport liquor during the day. *"We were in the 'logging business.' We put liquor in the trucks with logs. Hauling liquor with logs. That's just one of the deals we had.*" Though the details as to how a full-size school bus ended up in John Dewey's possession are unknown, it did make an ingenious cover for hauling liquor. *"I don't think we had a bus driver in the family."* Sometimes luck trumped any strategy. *"We had an old Studebaker we used to run liquor. We'd put the liquor in the back and put blankets over it. It must have been from the early '30s, standard color. One time a guy who was driving for John Dewey had a flat tire near Casey High School. Right next to the school was a service station with a night watchman. The driver had a flat tire right there and the night watchman came along and helped him fix that tire. He didn't say a word about the liquor in the back seat."*

Close calls did not stop Dewey. The operation spearheaded by him was a serious business that supported many people. *"We were wholesalers. We would sell by the load. Hell yes, it was profitable. That's why everyone risked their life to do it. The old man had a lot of mouths to feed. But we got a new car every year—Aunt Belle did. They'd just bring it out and she'd get a new Chevrolet every spring."*

With profits flowing, there was enough money to provide a little extra insurance that some law enforcement officers would look the other way. *"It was 1937. I know that because this highway patrolman had a new car, brand new 1937 Ford. It was a special deal for highway patrolmen because they had a pan underneath for airflow. Make 'em slick for high speed. My cousin and I took that highway patrol car from the big house and drove it to where we had the liquor hid, with his permission, oh yeah. We picked him up a bunch of liquor and put it in the back of the car. Me and my cousin, we took turns driving. It was a hot-rod deal. We drove a little bit farther than we needed to."*

Not every officer of the law could be bribed, and soon after Royce started working with John Dewy, his step-uncle's luck ran out. *"When the old man was in the penitentiary, Aunt Belle ran the business. We had another guy running the still. In the mornings before we went to school, Zu and I had to take the liquor down to the pasture and hide it. Ten-gallon kegs. We were keeping the liquor in a recess in the field. We would take a gunny sack, put hand holes in the side, and we'd carry that ten-gallon can and hide it during the day back in the field. That was our job to do that. We needed to hide it. Couldn't just leave it sittin' around."*

John Dewey Reeder served his sentence and returned home. His time in jail had not deterred him. In fact, his business only grew. With a high volume of liquor to distribute, he needed fearless young men to help him transport his product. Royce was now old enough to play a big role in this notorious part of the business. Though initially denied by NASCAR, it is now widely accepted that it was the bootleggers in the South that inspired, and in some cases supplied, early drivers in the sport. *"In those days, if you could outrun the law, you were free."* Outrunning police officers on back roads with sharp turns and often poor visibility resulted in some outstanding driving skills of the young bootleggers. They also learned a few things about how to make their cars go faster.

John Dewey and seventeen-year-old Royce hauled liquor in a 1940 Ford Coupe. *"We had a mechanic shop that we went to. The mechanic, Bill Gisentiner, I guess I can say his name now, had a shop right across the street from the whore house in Columbia. There was a coffee bar right next to the garage, kind of a restaurant. I would wait in there while Gisentiner worked on the car. He installed over-load springs on the car so it wouldn't sit down like it was loaded with liquor. We had special four-ply tires. We shaved the block to make the car faster. We had to go a hundred miles an hour. That's what it had on the speedometer and I've seen it lay over there lots of times. We had good brakes. We had a starter button, not a key. We had to be able to start quickly, a hot-start. We had a spotlight, the kind like the highway patrol used. It was mostly for the nights down in Georgia. The farmers didn't fence their pastures there and the cattle would lay on the asphalt at night. You could see their eyes a long way with that light. We'd run with that light on."*

The ability to go faster was not the only modification. *"Our mechanic would take the engine head off and drill that cylinder head back out of the block. He'd screw a pipe right on that cylinder head then run a pipe from there to the floorboard of the car on the front passenger side. This pipe went into a square pan about twelve-by-twelve. In that pan we put motor oil and hot pepper. It was to make smoke to burn your eyes. There was a valve right there with* a tube goin' off it into that cylinder head into the top of the piston. So, when we go to smoke, we open this valve and the oil goes right into the piston. The person sittin' in the passenger seat, well, that was me, would open that valve when the cops started to chase us. Hell yes, it worked. But it was a penitentiary offense if they caught ya' with one of those son-of-a-bitch pans in your car. It was so dangerous, see, of smokin' somebody while running at high speed. If you're smokin' somebody, it blinds 'em. And then they wreck. But the cops don't chase you if they see you got a can. Then they slow down and quit chasin' ya. Hell yes, I knew this was a penitentiary offense. The old man had been in the pen twice. I was a minor. That was the only ace-in-the-hole for me."*

There were other ways to disperse the homemade pepper spray, but John Dewey preferred to use the cylinder head valve system. "You could put the pepper and oil right into the exhaust pipe, but it has to be hot to work right. We wanted to be ready to go right when we jumped in the car." The passage of seventy decades since he last outran the police has not eliminated Royce's awareness of the serious trouble he could have been in. His recollection of this part of his past is uncharacteristically hazy. *"I don't remember if we used the smoke...we just puffed it a little bit...I don't remember it exactly...anyway."*

Like Reeder, Royce was not able to avoid getting in trouble with the law. *"The first time I was caught I was just in the car with the other driver. I wasn't scared a bit. It was a thin deal anyway."* And like his step-uncle, a close call didn't deter him from Reeder's business. Royce's mother and Aunt Belle were worried for Royce and tried to convince him he could make money in other ways. It was suggested to him that he take a job in the nearby textile mill. A lot of people were doing exactly this. By the 1930s, approximately seventy percent of all cotton textile production had moved from the north to southern states where workers could be employed for less money. At this time, only whites were hired to work in the relatively-modern cotton mills. Textile strikes, which originated in the north, began to occur in South Carolina as well. When Royce was twelve, Governor Ibra C. Blackwood publicly declared he would deputize every South Carolina mayor, sheriff, peace officer, and citizen to stop the protests. He called out the National Guard with orders to shoot to kill any picketers trying to enter the mills. Tragically, the governor's violent proclamation was carried out, resulting in the deaths of seven textile strikers and many more wounded after an altercation at Honea Path, South Carolina.

"Mother worked in the cotton mill after I got to be a little older. Aunt Belle worked in the mill, too. Mother wanted me to get a job and go work in the cotton mill also. But of course, I was doing boot leggin', gamblin', then. High school then. They wanted me to quit high school and go to work in the cotton mill as a profession. I only went in one a couple times—bobbins, spools, weaving. I said, 'Mom, I can't work in the cotton mill.' She didn't push me on this."

Royce refused to leave high school to work in the cotton mill in Columbia, but there was something else that did make him change his mind about finishing high school at that point in his life. When Royce was a sophomore in high school, Uncle Reeder took him to a little local airport. His first plane ride was in a yellow Piper Cub. Royce was hooked. He decided that someday he wanted to join the Air Force. Not yet eighteen, Royce left high school for the Palmetto

School of Aeronautics in Columbia. After successfully completing the program in a year-and-a-half, Royce received an engine license to work on airplanes. He had found a new passion, but he did not give up his involvement in Reeder's illegal business, at least not yet.

The moonshine business in the South was growing and so was the Federal Government's response. The Internal Revenue Service wanted to shut down alcohol producers that were not paying taxes. The Alcohol Tax Unit, ATU, headed by an IRS Deputy Commissioner in the United States Treasury Department, sent men into the field to destroy illegal stills and arrest those running them.

The ATU faced an uphill battle. Local law enforcement, prosecutors, and jury members often refused to punish moonshiners and bootleggers. *"I didn't like the law. They broke three or four of my stills up. They were always on the lookout. The head guy who worked for the Treasury Department out of Columbia would drive by Uncle Reeder's farm. He must a' noticed the drunk hogs. We would feed 'em mash left over from the still. Damned hogs be drunk by the fence. He was always chasin' our ass."*

Royce found out firsthand the determination of the ATU. *"I was a teenager running a still with an older guy. He was the strongest man I ever knew, about 35 at the time, a very knowledgeable stiller. We set up a still in a thicket near a pond. We fired the still up before daylight. We were usin' wood and didn't want the smoke to be seen. The ol' man decided to walk around in the woods to make sure it was safe. The grove had slicked leaves. When you walk on them, they turn over. He saw turned-over leaves and knew someone was in there. He came back to the still and real loud says, 'Let's go out and get some wood.' He gave me a sign and I knew there were agents waitin' to jump. As soon as we got out of the woods and into the clear we ran like hell. We had to cross a log across a stream. My old man (Uncle Reeder) couldn't sleep that night. He'd got in his car and was drivin' around to see what's goin' on. He was drivin' down a little road, white sand, ruts. There were bushes on either side. We saw John Dewey coming by and we just popped out of those bushes. He was within twenty feet of us! We ran to his car, each opened a side door and jumped into the car. We drove along and saw the Treasury Department guys' cars sittin' in the field. They tore that still up. We'd only run it once or twice."*

Royce's luck in running from the Treasury Department eventually ran out. After seventy-four years of absolute secrecy, he shares his final encounter on the wrong side of the law. *"I got a confession to make to ya'. I was seventeen years old. I was workin' with two other older guys on a still quite a ways from home. The three of us were workin' and all of the sudden the damn law came in, four or five guys from the Treasury Department, shootin' their guns in the air. We were down in a valley. I took off runnin' up the hill through the bushes and this guy who'd been hiding in the bushes jumped out and tackled me. They knew we'd try to run out; they'd been hidin' there after we got flushed out. I gave up after I was tackled. Watched 'em tear up our still. That was sickening to me. The drove us off in separate cars. On the way to Columbia, a thirty-minute drive or more, they stopped at a service station and asked me if I wanted a Coca-Cola. I said, 'No, I don't care for one.' They took me into their offices and questioned me pretty hard. They knew I was Reeder's boy. They thought I was his son.*

I told them, 'I know him, but he's got nothin' to do with this.' The sheriff who was always chasing me all the time, he said, 'Lock him up!' I don't think they handcuffed me. They put me in jail with another prisoner, a young guy who had been arrested for robbery. I had a nice black leather jacket on. He told me, 'Tonight you'd better sleep in your shoes and your jacket. If you don't, in the morning they'll be gone.' So I went to sleep with my jacket on. In the morning the bondsman came down and bailed me out. My trial didn't come up for a long time. I was concerned that if I had a record that would keep me out of the service."

Royce had been arrested by officers who were well aware of his stilling and bootlegging operations. Despite his distaste for the law, it appears that young Royce found sympathy from those in power. The judge handling Royce's case was concerned that Royce, an obviously very bright and enterprising young man, was headed down the wrong road. The judge's concern was dead right. As an older teenager, Royce found himself surrounded with other young men trying to stir up trouble. One of these men, Percy Shumpert, was an occupant of the boarding home

Royce's mother was running in Columbia. *"He was the driver of the truck that hauled the payroll for Fort Jackson. Just him and another guy, an officer on the payroll. They only had one gun with 'em. And he had it picked out where he could really bump the guy off. He wanted me to hold 'em up. I drew the line there. That same winter somebody threw Shupert off the train between Columbia and Miami and killed him."*

By the age of seventeen, Royce had survived his childhood, and in many ways, not all of them positive, had flourished. But now, with a birthday nearing that would bring with it legal adulthood, he knew he had to change his lifestyle. With the threat of violating the terms of his bond hanging over him, Royce stopped producing and distributing illegal alcohol. His attention turned to getting into the service, and he asked his step-uncle for help. Uncle Reeder hired an attorney to represent Royce and the adults worked out an offer that would keep Royce's record clean. In the judge's chambers, Royce was told he could *"clean the slate up"* if he joined the service, the exact deal Royce wanted to hear. The judge had been made aware of Royce's training to work on plane engines. Such an offer probably wasn't that unique at the time. *"Everybody began to talk about that the service was the place to go. And I wanted to go into the Air Force."*

When Royce enlisted in October of 1942, the United States was in its second year of mandatory draft registration for white males. Black men were registered for the draft a year after Royce's enlistment.

In the month of Royce's enlistment, three thousand Jews were murdered in Dubno, Russia. Sixteen thousand were killed in Pinsk later in the month. In Piotrkow, Poland, a thousand Jews were awoken from their sleep and sent to Treblinka where they were shot to death. This same month, over ten thousand Jews were transferred from Buchenwald concentration camp to Auschwitz. Over fifteen hundred citizens of Holland were gassed here shortly after. On the eighteenth of the month, Hitler ordered all captured Allied Commandos be killed.

Meanwhile, in the judicial chambers of a district magistrate judge in Richland County, South Carolina, an eighteen-year-old Royce Fulmer gladly made the decision to start out with a clean slate. *"I wasn't really that excited about joining the service, but I liked airplanes. That was the exciting part about it."*

CHAPTER 4
The Making of a Soldier

"I plowed all my life. I always started steppin' with my right foot down in the furrow. My drill sergeant pulled me out to learn to march. I needed to start marchin' with my left foot!"

R.A.F.

Royce's enlistment in the United States Armed Services was evidence that his childhood was officially behind him. He now found himself in basic training in a *"little ol' training field"* in his boyhood backyard of Columbia. Fort Jackson had been established during the First World War and had impressed Winston Churchill who inspected the fort just four months before Royce's arrival in June of 1942. Many practices of the Fort were distasteful to new enlistee Fulmer.

"When we got to Fort Jackson, they cut off our hair. That was nasty. I didn't like that at all. They really took charge, the transition to military life. Old sergeant was on my ass all the time. I think he could spot that I was a smart ass. I woke up that first morning before daylight and thought, 'Oh shit!' I was thinkin' about leavin'. But I decided I was going to stick it out. I'm not sure just what it was. I had a conversation in my head about this. The first morning in the Air Force, the Sergeant, he lined us up. Gave us an aluminum tray, cup. There was a pile of white sand. That's how we cleaned our mess kit. Washed it, shined it in that water and sand. I got that figured out. Of course, I didn't smoke, but we had to pick up cigarette butts. It didn't get much better the first couple weeks. Walk, march, calisthenics. Water got in our tents, cots, three or four inches deep. The legs of our cots were wet, our shoes were wet."

Royce's natural skills would be instrumental in moving him to a situation better suited for his interests. Despite a personal suspicion of intelligence tests, *"I always say those things are slanted,"* Royce scored high on examinations given to him. He had already completed his certification at Palmetto as an engine mechanic. As a result, he was sent to school at Kessler Army Airfield in Biloxi, Mississippi. At the time Royce was there, maintenance of the B-17 and B-24 airplanes was a specialty of the Airfield. Royce spent four months at Kessler working on every part of the airplanes. *"They did place me in the right place where I knew what I was doing. At least I could ad-lib to do stuff. Lived in the barracks. Livin' there was tough. Cot, couple blankets, footlocker. It would rain like hell down there."*

At the time construction began in 1941, Kessler was the largest federally funded project ever built in Mississippi. The training field was still under construction when Royce arrived. *"The sidewalks weren't even in, so they used oyster shells for walks."* Royce started to find his stride in his new environment. *"I got to be in charge of a platoon, marching them to school and back. By now I could handle the marching. Sometimes we'd wade in water above our knees. I had to keep the men in formation before daylight. They were always dropping off, slipping behind the barracks. They would mess around, tryin' to hide and play in the water. Then they'd sit in school all day with wet feet."*

After six months of rainy weather on the Gulf Coast, Royce was sent to a place closer to home, Smyrna Army Airfield near Smyrna, Tennessee. It was here that Royce would become an expert regarding the care, operation, and training for the most-produced aircraft of all time—the B-24.

The first test flight of a B-24 aircraft took off from San Diego, California less than nine months after the prototype had been only an idea on blueprints. This four-engine plane with propellers the size of a man, was jeered at by airmen who thought it was ugly compared to the sleeker B-17. For its time, the B-24 was mammoth in size. Its wings spread 110 feet. It was over 66 feet long and the plane reached a height of nearly 18 feet. With Pratt and Whitney engines, the plane could reach a speed of 300 miles per hour and climb to an altitude of 35,000 feet. The exterior of the B-24 had a design uniquely its own. On the end of the tail were two vertical stabilizers that gave the airplane its distinctive look. The plane had a tricycle landing gear design. There was one wheel under the nose with the two main wheels under the wings. The exterior shell of the plane was made of aluminum that could be cut with a sharp knife and shredded by German artillery.

The B-24 airplane was designed around the two bomb bays located on the belly of the plane. Operating like a roll-top desk, a single misstep on the door could cause it to open inflight. This was a real possibility; the interior of the plane was so cramped that only a narrow catwalk about eight inches wide existed for the men to get from one end of the plane to the other. It was tough just getting into the plane in the first place. Some crew members would climb up through a nose wheel well. Other crewmen climbed into the plane through open bomb bay doors three feet off the ground.

The B-24 went through a long series of modifications. It became a multi-purpose airplane for the United States and its allies. During World War II, every branch of the U.S. Armed Services employed this plane. The first B-24s were produced for Great Britain and France, though by the time the planes were ready, France was under German occupation. The planes, all of them now going to Great Britain, were labeled "The Liberator."

Much was asked of this plane and it delivered. The B-24 was capable of longer flights than its predecessors. Called the "workhorse" of the American Air Corps, this four-engine plane could stay in the air longer and carry more cargo than any other airplane in the fleet at that time. It was the only plane that could complete a nonstop flight across the Atlantic.

The U.S. Armed Forces wanted to increase production of the B-24 on a massive scale and sought private industry's help in producing the plane. The Ford Motor Company saw the opportunity and jumped in. From 1942-1945, Ford shut down civilian car production. Henry Ford ordered the construction of a mile-long plant on a track of land called Willow Run near Ypsilanti, Michigan. At the peak of its production, the plant, which produced almost half of the 18,000 B-24s built, could assemble a Liberator in 59.34 minutes. Record breaking production time was not the only achievement at the plant. Mr. Ford, not known for his tolerance for unions or integrating his workforce with women, changed his position on female workers probably due to a shortage of men as a result of the draft. The iconic "Rosie the Riveter" image was evidence that women could do jobs traditionally held only by men. Every Liberator produced required 700,000 rivets, many of which were punched by hand. These rivets literally held the airplane together.

It took incredible skill to operate and fly the B-24. Training of the pilots for this plane was more complex and took longer than other contemporary aircraft. The plane required physical strength from the pilot and co-pilot just to operate the controls. Preparing for combat, the pilots trained in heavy bombardment tactics by flying in tight formations. They learned how to keep their planes in the air when damaged by enemy fire; they practiced flying the four-engine plane on three, and then two engines.

The B-24 was known by many names, most of them not flattering. "The Flying Box Car," "The Flying Coffin," "Flying Brick," "Flying Cow," "The Old Army Wagon," "Spam in a Can," and Royce Fulmer's own description, *"...it was a whistling shit house. It was the ugliest airplane the Air Force had. It had big ol' twin tails. It could go high altitude or low altitude. It was a good airplane, no question about it. It could carry twice the bomb load the B-17 did. The B-24 could slow down and we could fly it at low altitude and stall like we were coming in for a landing and drag it along."*

It took a lot of training to teach the young man from rural South Carolina how to make that huge plane respond to his command. After intense training and hands-on experience with the B-24, Royce found himself rising to the top of a diverse group of young men. *"I went up pretty fast. Got along pretty good with aeronautics. . . One nice thing about the draft, all kind of people there. People who came out of big, rich families. Poor kids too, of course."*

At the age of nineteen, Royce had a new job in the Armed Services; he was an assistant flight engineer for the B-24 Liberator. The engineer for a B-24 knew more about the airplane than any of his crewmates. Standing on the raised deck between the pilot and co-pilot during takeoff, and often while in the air, the flight engineer was the man the pilot, who was the commander of the plane, would turn to in an emergency. The flight engineer was responsible for the safe operation of the plane, closely monitoring its complex and unpredictable systems. He monitored how the engines were performing and kept track of how much fuel was being used, information that could mean the difference between life and death. *"I would walk all around the airplane, checking the bomb bay there, the oxygen, all the systems."* Flight engineers also had the extra duty of being a gunner in the top turret, a position that allowed them to visually inspect the plane's four engines. *"Sometimes I was up in the top turret. I operated that when we had the possibility of a problem."*

To his dismay, Royce would not be assigned immediately to a combat crew. His skills were thought by those in charge to be better served working with new pilots during their training. It wasn't until after World War II that the Air Force became its own separate branch of the United States military. In the two years before Royce's enlistment in 1942, the Army, containing the Army Air Corps, had a membership of only 26,000 men. Given the small numbers to start, and the high causality rate in combat, there was great need for new pilots. Royce stayed at Smyrna and trained these green pilots. *"I flew with the pilots all the time in the B-24; got 'em ready for combat. Once in a while we'd have two officers in there. It could be pretty rough. I was in charge of the landing gear, all the emergency procedures on the plane. If something happened, not work exactly right, then I was there to help them."*

Instructor pilots would fly with the pilots in training, but eventually the time would come for the new pilots to fly on their own. As an engineer on these training flights, Royce would remain with the novice pilots when they made their first solo flights. *"One time an instructor pilot got out of the plane and told me to stay with them. The two training pilots were crying that they were scared. They didn't think they were ready to fly on their own. The instructor looked at me and said, 'Sarge, what do you think?' I said, 'Oh, I think we can handle it.' That made them feel a little better."* Even though he had not had formal flight instruction himself, Royce wasn't concerned. *"Oh, I knew how to fly the son-of-a-bitch...I hadn't had a formal flight class, but I had absorbed it. I was flying six hours a day there."* Royce's confidence rubbed off on the two young pilots. *"We taxied out to take off. I told 'em, 'No sweat. You guys can handle it.' It was a little scary at first. We had four engines; these kids were out of twin-engine trainers. We took off and we circled the field and if I remember right, we made a pretty damn good landing."* It didn't take long for the new pilots' outward confidence to match their skills. *"There was a place in Nashville where these kids were from and the officers would go there. These two kids got cocky and buzzed that place. A couple of landings and they got cockier than shit."*

Royce was living his dream of flying in airplanes at the air base in Tennessee. Even though he was the assistant crew chief, he found himself in the air nearly every day because his crew chief didn't like to fly. His crew chief's reluctance seems unusual. During World War II, the Armed Services never forced anyone to fly. Every man who flew had made that choice for himself. Logging lots of flight hours, however, wasn't the only fun nineteen-year-old Royce was having. *"I was really having a good time. Gambled a lot there—craps. Shooting craps, very basic craps. Not a big spread like Vegas. Obviously, I came out a little ahead. We'd play on the base at night. We got caught by the MP, and he sent us to the squadron commander."*

Perhaps Royce's skills as an instructor helped get him off the hook from punishment for illegally gambling on the base. Regardless, being caught once was not enough to deter him from continuing to play. Like the problem he faced being caught a second time running moonshine, the second offense for being caught playing craps had consequences as well. And like the time in the judge's chambers, Royce actually didn't mind the consequence. *"About the time I got caught playing craps the Memphis Belle had come through our base. They were on tour and stopped there. It was a big deal. They got all this publicity. I just wanted to go to combat and fly with the combat crews. Well yes, I wanted to be a 'hot shot,' I just don't like to put it that way."*

After being caught the second time for playing craps Royce proposed a solution. *"I said, I want to go to combat. The squadron commander said 'okay,' cause they needed guys real bad."* Volunteering for a mission where the odds of dying were high did not worry Royce. *"I was never afraid. I don't know why. When you go through what I went through as a kid, shit doesn't scare you too much. I had seen knife fights and everythin' else. The sharecroppers use to fight with knifes when they got mad with each other. One neighbor was a World War I vet. I saw him cut another man. I was less than ten years old."*

With the order to become part of a combat crew, Royce had to learn a new skill; how to shoot a gun while flying in a plane. Royce was sent to gunnery school at Tyndal Field, twelve miles east of Panama City, Florida. Sixty-one thousand men would train at this base built on top of white sand and swamp land. *"Clark Gable was there. I saw him. He went through school there; he was three weeks ahead of me. He flew a combat mission or two, but then got into photography. Girls would just piss their pants when they saw him. He wore clothes just like the rest of us. People would point him out a little bit. He lived in the officer barracks. I never did go for that movie star bit, except for Jimmy Stewart. He was a squadron commander. I heard a lot about him because he flew combat missions. He didn't mess around with any Clark Gable stuff."*

Movie stars aside, the business of the gunnery school was serious. The men had to learn how to accurately shoot in a moving plane at high altitudes out of open windows. *"We started shooting skeet first. We'd shoot a box of twenty-four shells each. Our shoulders would get so black and blue we'd put newspaper on our shoulders. Of course, there was no ear protection. We did it all day long. They were rushin' us through there to send us to combat. There was a tower twenty-feet tall with a turret in it. That's where they'd throw the skeet. We went from hand-held guns to 50-caliber guns. That one you couldn't hold; it had to be in the gun turret."*

After gaining experience shooting skeet from the tower, the men were moved to a second phase of their training. *"We had a shot gun and rode in a truck through a trail in the woods. We wouldn't know where the skeet would be shootin' from. Every truck would get one big clay pigeon that would fall in the back of the truck."*

After their skills were honed on the ground, it was time to take their training to the air. *"There were canvas targets pulled by airplanes for target practice. They'd be pulled by AT-6 planes. All the gunners had a different paint color tip so you could see if the gunner hit the target. Yes, I passed. This was the final for graduation. As long as you didn't hit the goddamn pilot pulling the target, you graduated!"*

The pilot pulling Royce's target survived the training and Royce was ready to go to Colorado Springs, Colorado. It was there he would be assigned to the B-24 crew that would make him a World War II combat airman.

CHAPTER 5
"Crewin' Up!"

In the spring of 1944, nineteen-year-old Royce Fulmer took a train from Panama City, Florida and headed to the Rocky Mountains. His destination was Peterson Army Air Base just outside of Colorado Springs. This airbase sprung out of an arid Colorado field, displacing sage brush, jack rabbits, and rattlesnakes. Originally a photo reconnaissance training school, Pete Field was now used to assemble and train B-24 crews for combat. Hundreds of Liberator combat crews would go through the one-to-three-month training required of them.

The first significant thing to happen to Royce at Pete Field was to find out who would be in his combat crew. Typically, the B-24 Liberator flew daytime bombing raids with a crew of ten men. At this point, Royce and the other men he would soon meet had no reason to believe their experience would be any different. As the flight engineer, Royce was the leader of the enlisted men which included the radio operator and gunners. Royce recalls *"standing around, talkin' with his guys"* just before they were told who their pilot would be. Pilots, co-pilots, navigators, and bombardiers were always officers. Before the crews were named, the officers would stand to one side of a large platform, the enlisted men on the other. *"There was a guy on a big platform, and he would say, 'Group so and so, meet over there by the wall,' for instance. They were callin' out pilot's names and they'd get on the platform. Good lookin' son-a-bitches, caps crushed back. Swagger. Looked like hot shots. Except there was one pilot who had on a fuzzy green cap, the only one in the whole goddamn bunch with that kinda' cap. He wasn't very tall, about five-foot-seven. He was the most un-cool of the whole bunch. He looked like a nerd. I laughed and told my* guys, *'See that guy with the green cap on? That's gonna be our pilot!' I'd been training these guys. I wanted a hot shot pilot, not a guy who didn't have a crushed cap.*"

The man with the wool cap, not the sleeker gabardine kind admired by Royce, was William Liscum Borden. He would, in fact, become the pilot of Royce's crew. "*When they announced that he was gonna' be our pilot, we was just pissed. But that guy was a brain. How they fit us together was just perfect. I was training see; I had been a crew chief, so I knew right away in our training that he was a hell of a pilot. Come to find out it was a perfect match. He was smart. He'd been to Yale. He could fly, but he didn't know anything about the airplane. That was my department. We was such a team together because I respected his knowledge and he respected mine.*"

Borden, three years older than Royce, was born in Washington D.C. in 1920 to Daniel and Pauline Borden. "*He was just rich; he smelled rich, ya' know?*" The oldest of three sons, he lived in a home that in 1930 was valued at $20,000. Today that value could easily reach over four million dollars. The

Borden children lived in their home on Woodlawn Drive in the nation's capital with their parents and two "servants." The "maid," Catherine E. Henderson, was born in Maryland. The "nurse," who was assigned the responsibility of caring for the children, was Alice Tabor. She was from Switzerland and spoke French. Royce is certain Borden spoke the language as well. At the time Borden enlisted as a private in the Army Air Corps in April of 1942, he was twenty-four years old. He had graduated from Yale, he was single, and he listed his occupation as "actor." His enlistment records show he was actually an inch taller than Royce recalls; he was five-foot-eight. Like nearly all the men flying in tight quarters of Air Corps planes, he was thin, weighing just 153 pounds.

Royce quickly grew to respect Borden. *"We flew several practice missions together out of Peterson Field. I knew he was a good pilot. Didn't take me very long to figure that out. I was impressed with his calmness. I was damned impressed after a while. I could tell he was a winner, I really could. He didn't drink, smoke, curse. He wasn't rowdy. He was levelheaded. He didn't talk about his background. He gave me his liquor rationing and cigarette card which I gave to the crew. I didn't drink or smoke either."*

The draft during World War II brought together men from all backgrounds. Because of their youth, they did not yet have a lot of life experience as adults. They did, however, represent a variety of economic and cultural experiences. Vernon L. Doran was the co-pilot for the Borden Crew. Doran came from the Kansas prairie. Growing up on a family farm in Stafford County, Doran's childhood was surrounded by grass-covered sand dunes and the largest inland saltwater marsh in the United States. Now preserved as the Quivira National Wildlife Refuge, hundreds of thousands of migratory birds pass through this part of Kansas every fall enticing tourists from all over the nation to visit a county which still does not allow the sale of alcohol. Doran decided to attend Kansas State University and graduated from the College of Agriculture and Applied Science in 1938. After college, he returned to work on the family farm before his enlistment. *"Doran was a good fit with Borden. They fit great together, really. He was just a nice guy."* Doran was one of two married men on the crew, and at the age of 27, was the second oldest.

The pilot of the aircraft was the man in charge. He was the officer responsible for the safety of his crew both in the air and on the ground. The pilot's primary job was to get the plane to the target and return to base, or if necessary, find a safe place to land the plane. It was the pilot who made split-second calls in times of emergencies. The co-pilot served as the pilot's assistant, and had flight training as comprehensive as the pilot's. As the pilot's executive officer, the co-pilot was prepared to take over the plane if the pilot was hurt or killed in flight.

The third officer on the flight crew was the navigator, Jack P. Barton. It was his job to keep the plane on course to its destination, giving the pilot compass headings. He was to know where the plane was at all times. A navigator could have no fear of mathematics. He needed to be well-versed in plane geometry and spherical trigonometry. This background gave him the skill set to use a variety of means to determine location. Sitting on a tiny retractable stool behind the cockpit, and at a lower level where he could see only the pilot's feet, the navigator's small table held the papers containing his charts. The basic method used to determine location was dead reckoning—keeping track of the distance the plane had flown from its last-known position. Celestial navigation, determining location from calculations made using two-star constellations, was an important navigational tool when flying over water.

Barton was well-qualified to keep the Borden Crew flying in the right direction. He had entered college at the age of sixteen. Born in Whitney, Texas, the oldest of five children, education was a priority in the Barton family. His mother was a schoolteacher in a number of school districts in central and northern Texas. Barton would become a graduate of Texas A&M. Established in 1871, A&M is the oldest public institution of higher learning in Texas, though this history is not as deep as the Barton family. The first Bartons arrived in America in 1654. In the early years of the University, enrollment at A&M was restricted to men only who would participate in the Corps of Cadets, the student military organization. This early history was instrumental in producing twenty thousand troops for deployment in World War II. More officers came out of Texas A&M during the War than the U.S. Military Academy and Naval Academy combined.

After graduating from A&M in 1943, Barton attended flight school at the University of Tennessee. Other graduates of this program included the Tuskegee Airmen and female pilots who flew for the Women's Air Force Service or WASPS. Royce recalls that Barton was *"sharper than shit. He could navigate by the stars. He'd shoot pic shots going overseas, used an instrument for navigation. He was good at that."*

The final officer of the Borden Crew was the bombardier, James D. Bruning. Bombardiers were trained to work with the pilot and co-pilot to determine the point at which to drop the explosives. Such decisions required the bombardier to make calculations that factored in altitude, air speed, type of bomb dropped, wind drift, and air density. These decisions were improved with the introduction of one of the most closely protected military secrets of the time, the Norden Bombsight. An oath was required of those that operated this high-tech piece of equipment, requiring that they swear to be "mindful of the fact that I am to become guardian of one of my country's most precious military assets..." The secrecy level was clear to Royce. *"Bruning had to escort that bombsight out to the plane with MPs. That was a new thing. The Norden Bombsight corrected for everything. It took over the airplane. When you get on a bomb run then the pilots are hands off. Portable deal. I didn't see it because I didn't use the bombs, but I knew what was goin' on. As a bombardier, Bruning could have been a leader of a group of us."*

At the time the Borden Crew was assembled and began their training, Bruning had no way of knowing that his duties in combat would be much different than most other bombardiers. Like Royce, Bruning was from the South, born in Louisville, Kentucky. One of four siblings, his father died from cancer when all the children, very close in age, were also very young. Rather than separate to other families as Royce's family had done, extended family came to live with and support the young Brunings. His early life was full of cousins and playing in the Ohio River. At the time he took the oath to protect one of America's most secret weapons, he was no more than twenty years old.

The rest of the Borden Crew was made up of enlisted men. In a typical Liberator crew there were ten men. However, two men, both gunners whom

Royce cannot recall by name, would not be needed for the Borden Crew's mission. They were re-assigned. That left Royce as flight engineer, two gunners, and a radio operator as the enlisted side of the crew. The radio operator on the Borden Crew was Max E. Dinsmore. The "old man" of the group, Dinsmore was born in 1910. He was 34 when he flew with the Borden Crew. Dinsmore lived in several Midwestern states. Originally from Iowa, he claimed Missouri as his home state at the time of his enlistment. He was married and made his living as a farm hand. He had personal knowledge of the physical toll of combat. His stepfather, a man from Kansas whose last name he took, had fought in France during the First World War at the battles of Meuse Argonne and St. Mihiel. He was wounded several times and never fully recovered from his exposure to poison gas that could penetrate crude masks.

The job of the radio operator was two-fold. He would sit in the cramped upper fuselage of the cockpit with his headset on and listen to static crackling in his ears. It was his job to give position reports to help the navigator with location. He was also the second waist gunner. Royce fondly recalls of Dinsmore, "*He was a hell-of-a nice old guy. He liked us too, called us 'youngins'. We called him 'Pappy' all the time 'cause he had 'Pappy' on his jacket, a nickname. He could have gotten out, but he decided to stay with the crew."*

The remaining enlisted men were gunners. Like the rest of the Borden Crew, they would be assigned additional duties on their as-yet-unknown secret combat missions. Harry P. Kieschnick was another Texan on the Borden Crew. Twenty-three years before his birth in 1924, his home county of Jefferson had experienced an oil explosion at Spindletop Hill. For over a week in 1901, oil gushed from the ground rising into the air more than two hundred feet high. The county became the site of the first major oil field in the United States. With a year of college, Kieshnick was nineteen years old when he joined the crew. His occupation before the war was listed as "clerk, general office" and he could speak German fluently, a skill which would serve the entire crew in the months to come. *"He was a sharp guy, very intelligent."*

The other gunner on the crew was Stacy V. Phillips. Ten months younger than Royce, Phillips left his parents, brother, and three sisters to enlist when he was eighteen. With a father who was an electrical engineer working for the Ohio Power Company, Phillips had been a serious student and athlete. He was the star running back on several championship football teams in high school as well as a competitive swimmer and basketball player. Though college and a distinguished career as an educator would come after the war, his first experience after high school graduation was as a student at the Fort Bliss gunnery school in El Paso, Texas. Phillips is the only crew member other than Royce still living at the time of this writing.

Phillips was the tail gunner on the Borden Crew. *"He was just a sharp guy. He handled his job well. He didn't complain. He wasn't late. He was the first gun, in the tail gun."* After the completion of their combat duties in World War II, it would be sixty-nine years before the two men would reconnect. In a phone call arranged for them, the two men's memories of each other were vivid. Phillips recalls with a chuckle, "Royce was a gambler. He and I were going to buy a race car after the war."

Royce estimates that by the time he started flying with the Borden Crew, he had four to five thousand flight hours from training others to fly the B-24. This was substantially more experience than most Air Corps men in the air at that time. The process of teaching these crews how to fly in their airplanes was itself dangerous. In 1943, eight hundred and fifty airmen in B-24 crews died in training before they had even left the States. The Borden Crew would have less than ten training flights before they went overseas. Despite their short time together, they felt confident in each other and quickly bonded as a team. *"We had about five practice missions out 'a Colorado. We were getting familiar with the airplane and the crew with each other. We checked each other out."*

As a last good-bye to his family, Pilot Borden asked his crew for a favor. *"He said he would like to buzz his folk's summer place on the lake. We went out on the lake and we lowered damned low. We were right on the treetops there anyway, probably 250-300 feet off the ground which would be a pretty good deal in that bomber. We shook the roof on that son-of-a-bitch when we flew over that house. We were going into combat. Hell, we were on our way."*

One major question was still unanswered. The crew had yet to be told if they would be going to a warm, or cold and rainy climate to fight. *"We didn't know if we were gonna go to Europe or the South Pacific. We flew to a supply depot in Dayton, Ohio. When we got our clothes, we knew where we were going. We had fleece-lined clothes. We knew then we were headed to Europe."*

With sheep-lined leather bomber jackets, hats, boots, and gloves, the Borden Crew flew to the nearly sub-arctic climate location where they would take off for Europe. They arrived at Goose Bay, a province of Newfoundland and Labrador in an area that today is in Canada. With short, mild summers that last only a few weeks, this part of the world can easily see a hundred and eighty inches of snow a year. By 1942, the triangularly-shaped base with gravel runways was jammed with airplanes landing and refueling on the way to the United Kingdom. When Royce arrived, he felt like *"we were in the boonies up there. It was sixty-five degrees below zero!"*

The crew would spend just one cold night in Goose Bay before their flight across the Atlantic. The plan was to fly in a loose formation with ten other B-24 crews to Meeksfield, Iceland. The over-water journey, at a distance of more than 1,600 miles, was expected to take ten hours. These trips were made in groups, as the end of the flight could encounter trouble. *"They were flyin' in groups there so not to be shot down in the North Sea. There were trollers, disguised German boats that would try to shoot down our bombers."*

Even if the airplanes avoided combat, just navigating to their destination was difficult. To help ensure they would find their final destinations, a group of airplanes would cross the ocean together. The pilot and crew of the first plane to take off would serve as lead navigators responsible for setting the flight path for the entire group of airplanes flying together across the Atlantic. Knowing the next day they might have their first experience with combat, the crew settled in to rest. The officers were in one barrack, the enlisted men in another. On the morning of their take off to Europe, Royce and the other enlisted men got to the plane before the officers. The first men to the plane would pull the propellers to get the engine started. The engines ran for a solid ten minutes in the freezing cold. The officers were still missing. Regardless of rank, the comfort of warm blankets on a cold, dark morning can be difficult to leave. When the other nine Liberator crews took off in formation to cross the Atlantic, Royce realized the leader of his airplane and all his officers had overslept. The other planes were on their way to Europe. Royce's crew was now completely on their own.

"I had the engines runnin', but then I shut them down when our pilot wasn't there. When he did get to the plane, he got his ass chewed royally. He was all upset. The other crews had already taken off. Our punishment was we were gonna have to fly all by ourselves to Iceland. That was the punishment."

The four engines of the B-24 were started up again by Flight Engineer Fulmer. He knew this could pose a problem. *"We got back in the airplane and started the engine. See, I'd already run this engine probably ten minutes and these big ol' engines had an exhaust pipe down there and oil would leak down in there occasionally. If run, it would leak down. Well, I made my check-up and I saw a little oil there, but we were in a hurry, so we took off."*

Royce's childhood experiences had taught him to trust his instincts. In this case, his concern about the hurried take off across the Atlantic would prove, once again, that his gut feeling was right.

CHAPTER 6
Off We Go

Royce had spent the last twenty-two months preparing crews for combat. Finally, he was a member of his own crew. As a flight engineer, he felt well-qualified to keep the Liberator in the air. It was his job to problem solve; he just never imagined one of those problems would be a pilot who over-slept.

The transatlantic flight was going to be difficult even in the best of circumstances. The Borden Crew's flight from Goose Bay, Labrador, to their destination at Meeks Field, Iceland, would take over ten hours, far longer than any of their training flights. The flying conditions these men faced contrasts greatly with an airplane ride across the Atlantic today. A modern commercial flight from New York City to Iceland is no more than six hours, complete with comforts we now demand as consumers. There was no warm food, toilets with seats, or in-flight entertainment for the Borden Crew.

In 1944, a flight across the Atlantic Ocean was potentially dangerous for young men heading to war. Primitive navigation systems increased the risk that an airplane could become lost and run out of fuel before reaching Europe. An observant navigator was critical. A slight navigational miscalculation at takeoff could grow during the long flight, causing the plane to reach the other side of the Atlantic far off its mark and possibly in hostile airspace. The crews had no option other than to ferry their planes to their destinations. A crash landing into the frigid North Atlantic would mean death within minutes to any survivors in the freezing water.

Harsh weather conditions across the Atlantic made flying even more dangerous than usual. Finicky carburetors could ice up in freezing temperatures. The U.S. government's operations manual for the B-24 states very clearly the problems of a frozen airplane, "Formation of this ice anywhere in the induction system can block off the flow of air to the engine and cause almost instantaneous engine failure." A watchful flight engineer was always critical to the safe operation of the airplane as underscored by the operation manual, "Icing can progress almost to the point of engine failure before it is indicated in your instruments unless you are alert."

Royce had survived his dangerous childhood precisely because he had learned the skill of always being alert. He was aware of his environment swinging from a cow's horns, running moonshine on dark roads, or now inside a B-24 Liberator that was crossing the Atlantic alone.

"We took out over the North Atlantic, over the ocean. We'd been in the air about thirty minutes. The damn gunner on the right side said, 'Fire in number two!' And that son-of-a-bitch, I looked out that window and flames were lappin' around the wings. Shit, there was fire five to ten feet on both sides of that wing. Borden looked at me and he was white. He grabbed for the goddamned fire extinguisher and I said, 'no, no, no.' That's what you would normally do, but I had another plan. I knew where the fire was coming from. I wasn't that dumb to start an engine again. That was in all the books; never re-start an

engine. Oil collected in the ring there. But now we were in the air and had to put out the damn fire. I told Skipper (Borden) to feather the prop, shut down the plane, open the cowl flaps, then dive it until the fire blew out. See, oil won't light easy once you've burned the gasoline out of your oil. It won't catch on fire again. We got that son-of-a-bitch back runnin'. Skipper got the prop to turnover slowly where you wouldn't damage the pusher rods in there. We started the engines up again and flew it to Iceland. Nobody ever knew we had a fire and kept the plane going. Yeah, we kept that to ourselves."

Standing between the pilot and copilot while instructing them how to put out the fire lasted, according to Royce's best estimate, a long five minutes. When asked what the rest of the crew was doing as their plane was on fire, Royce answered wryly, *"messin' their pants."* The successful extinguishing of the fire showed the crew the skill and calm demeanor of their flight engineer. *"We had only had five practice flights as a crew before we left for Iceland. When we got the fire put out, I made many points there. The crew saw I knew what I was doin'."*

The rest of the flight was uneventful, and thanks to Barton who had suddenly been promoted to de-facto lead navigator, the crew landed at their destination: Meeks Field, Iceland. *"We had no navigational instruments other than a radio. Barton had to take shots with an instrument out the window of the plane. He navigated us there by way of the planets and stars."*

The presence of Allied troops in Iceland had not been completely welcomed. This ancient land where Vikings began their voyages to the New World was full of fiercely independent people who were wary of the Allied Forces. But when Hitler attempted to expand his influence to the island in May of 1940, British and Canadian forces were reluctantly accepted. As German forces pushed hard in other areas of the world, Britain relocated their troops from Iceland, and the United States stepped in with a force of 30,000 men.

The construction of Meeks Field Airbase in July of 1942 was important for the United States. It was used as the main landing base for American planes coming to Europe. It was also a supply field for bomb squadrons. Americans fresh to the war would be assigned to fill in for existing crews who had lost crewmembers. Crews landing at this base were greeted by icebergs made visible by the Northern Lights. Though the terrain was far different from the backwoods of South Carolina, some things were very much the same. *"I'd bought some liquor in the States to bring with me. I didn't drink it. It was for bartering. We had all our fancy equipment and clothes in the airplane. I wanted to make sure everything was safe after we left the plane. I gave the guard a fifth of liquor. He was gonna be out in the cold, guardin' our plane."*

The Borden Crew spent several days at Meeks Field. *"We were studying during this time. We had a lot of things to talk about: the language, where we would probably go, how the bombers operated. We would go from here to a bombing outfit."* This was indeed the normal course, but for the Borden Crew this is where their path would be different. *"Our crew was taken into a room by ourselves. We were asked to volunteer for a special mission. We wasn't too eager for that. In the service you never volunteer for anything. Kennedy's brother had been killed on a special mission. I think they selected us because they knew we had come over by ourselves. That's what I think."*

At the time they were asked to accept the mission, the Borden Crew was given no details about what they would be asked to do. Lack of specifics did not prevent the crew from considering the offer. *"We had a lot of confidence. We felt we could do any damn thing."* After a short discussion between all the crew members, the offer was accepted. The crew waited nervously on the base at Meeks Field for three days before learning where they and their Liberator would be sent.

CHAPTER 7
Mission Revealed

"Our mission was a challenge, just like everything else in my life."

R.A.F.

After agreeing to participate in the mission that had not yet been explained to them, the Borden crew was transported to a secret base: "Station 179." This airfield, located eighty-three miles north of London, had been built by the United States Army in the summer of 1942. Surrounded by cattle farms and rolling pastures, the base had three runways. The main one was just a mile in length. The closest village to the base was Harrington, though the townsfolk were not allowed near the base and the men on base were not to talk to the residents about their work. "*We were warned not to talk about the mission. After the war, some of our guys helped start the C.I.A. We had a clearance, took an oath. Damned right I took that seriously.*"

Waiting at their new base, the Borden Crew was again divided by officers and enlisted men when it came to their sleeping arrangements. Royce and the other enlistees shared a Quonset Hut with another crew. These light-weight, prefabricated barracks provided greater protection from cold English winters compared to previous barracks: a tent with a wooden floor. The shelters were easily assembled with simple tools. Quonset Huts were first produced in Quonset Point, Rhode Island, a New England town that took its name from a Native American tribe that once lived there. To them, quonset meant boundary. The structures, which could be used for a variety of purposes, were made of corrugated galvanized steel shaped into a semi-circle. The ends were covered with plywood with cutouts for small windows. The front end had the building's only door. For Royce, the Quonset Hut made a cozy home.

"*There was a little coal stove in the middle of the hut to keep it heated. The base had a big coal pile with a fence around it. We would be issued a certain amount of coal. One of the guys on base would have guard duty around the perimeter of the base. Occasionally he'd throw a little extra coal over the fence for us to use. The floor in the Quonset was concrete and on either side of the door there was a wall reinforced with concrete. I took the spot closest to the door. I knew the Germans had used their fighter planes to strafe buildings. I wanted to be in an area where I was protected. We slept on metal cots. No mattresses, they had 'biscuits.' There were three of them, square shaped, on a cot. We would try to find parachutes after someone had to bail out and would use that as a sheet. The biscuits were horsehair. Scratchy as shit. It was just pretty damn nice. I would think about the infantry men who were sleeping in trenches and I realized we had a good situation.*"

Royce and his crew waited three days on their new base before the mission was explained to them. They shared their Quonset with another crew of enlisted men who maintained secrecy but delighted in teasing the novices. *"Normally there would have been three crews in a hut, but one of the crews was missing. The other guys who'd been flyin' would try to scare us at night, not tellin' us anything about the mission but just tryin' to worry us."* When Royce learned the specifics of the mission, there wasn't time for worry.

"We were called into a briefing. They told us we would be dropping spies and supplying the underground in France and other nearby countries. At night. That's what the concern was about. In fact, I was a little nervous about it. None of the regular bomber crews had any night training. And we would be flying at low altitudes at very slow speeds. After training with pilots for a year, I was very aware of the dangers of night flying. You'd be surprised at the number of pilots we lost just on training flights. They'd make flying or landing errors. Flying at night was much more difficult, even for the best of crews. It would be easy to fly into something, a hill, a mountain."

Royce knew every inch of the B-24 Liberator. So, at their first briefing, he became aware there was something unusual going on. *"They took us up to the flight line where the planes are parked. I immediately saw the differences in these Liberators. They were painted black. I noticed flame dampeners where the exhaust comes out so you couldn't see the exhaust as far at night. There was no nose turret or side guns, no ball turret. There were black curtains on the windows. This was going to be different. I knew we had to be well thought of to put us on our own. But Borden could fly that son-of-a-bitch plane. The bombardier, navigator, they were damned smart. It was just another thing that we were gonna get into."*

Royce's observations about the crew's new airplane showcase the many modifications made to the B-24 for the Carpetbagger Missions. On these missions, the airplanes would seek to avoid contact with the enemy. All guns except for the upper and tail turrets were removed, freeing up more room for cargo. This is why the crew was reduced from the usual ten to eight; the additional two gunners were not needed. The ball turret located in the belly of the airplane was removed and covered with plywood. The cover had a hinge down the middle that would fold back when the spies were getting in position to jump. The spies, called "Joes" and "Josephines," would sit on the smoothed edge of the hole. A strap secured to their jumpsuits would hold them in until a light positioned close to the "Joe Hole" would go from red to green. The crewman assigned to oversee the spies was called the dispatcher. He would have been the waist gunner in a normal crew. Like all Carpetbagger dispatchers, waist gunner Kieschnick, now assigned the position of dispatcher, was required to learn how to parachute. *"Kieschnick had to go to jump school in Ringway, Scotland. He had to do three jumps. He was the one who handled the spies."*

How Operation Carpetbagger Came Into Being...

Prior to World War II, the United States did not have a centralized intelligence agency. This changed with the creation of the Office of Strategic Services, OSS, in June of 1942. Within the OSS was a division called "Special Ops" that was assigned the task of preparing forces to conduct and defend against sabotage and guerilla warfare. When the U.S. entered the war, it was widely recognized that intelligence gathering would be critical in bringing about a successful invasion across the English Channel. In the spring of 1943, the U.S. and England established a formal invasion planning staff in London. A key component of these plans involved supporting special operations inside Nazi-occupied areas.

The Royal Air Force had already been using their airpower to make drops of supplies and agents. The British equivalent of the OSS, the Special Operations Executive (SOE), requested help. American airpower could supply heavy bombers capable of greater loads and could fly longer ranges. The U.S. Special Ops Division and Britain's SOE reached an agreement to work together, sharing headquarters in their joint effort to support the Resistance fighters. The OSS found themselves in need of airpower. They approached the U.S. Army Air Forces for help. After some negotiating between the War Department and the Department of the Navy, four squadrons of B-24s were provided by the Navy. In November of 1943, new special operations squadrons, 36th and 406th Bombardment, were formed.

The newly-assigned American crews needed special training to learn how to fly their airplanes in the unique conditions the operation required. Initially, training took place at the Royal Air Force base at Tempsford, England. On the first day of May 1944, Operation Carpetbagger moved to the base outside of Harrington, the base the Borden Crew would call home for seven months. The codename, "Operation Carpetbagger," did not have any particular meaning. Rather, it was the next name on a pre-determined list for secret missions for WW II. The name choice was much simpler than the actual mission. The goal of Operation Carpetbagger was straightforward: to supply Resistance fighters in Nazi-occupied territories with the tools they needed to help win the war.

The practical issues created by an operation that ultimately dropped over four and a half tons of supplies and nearly 1,000 people, required a large, well-organized support team. Everything had to be kept secret. Each man had only the information necessary to complete his job. The men were well aware of the consequences of being shot down. If captured "*we knew the enemy would have something a little extra for us.*" Royce and the other Airmen carried a small American pocket flag with them to prove what side they were on. If caught by the enemy, this flag would only condemn them. The men were not allowed to keep journals. Any letters sent home were censored by a commanding officer. Unlike the crews who flew daylight bombing raids, the victories of the Carpetbaggers were known only to a few.

How Operation Carpetbagger Worked...

For the eight members of the Borden crew, their mission began with a briefing which described a proposed mission. To get to this point in the operation cycle, hours of preparation by hundreds of people were required. Everything hinged on meeting the needs of the Resistance fighters. Phone calls or messages delivered by pigeons were directed to London from Resistance fighters outlining specific requests for supplies and agents. A call was then placed from London to Station 179. These messages were sent by code which, after being deciphered, were passed to the Operations Room. Working on a map taller than a man, the exact drop point for a mission was plotted. Weather conditions were always a concern. In fact, most of the missions were intentionally flown on moonlit nights in an effort to reduce the risk that the low-flying plane would collide with the landscape. Some missions, however, were flown in bad weather when Resistance forces desperately needed help. Weather wasn't the only factor in determining what drop zone to accept. Enemy artillery was a constant threat and needed to be avoided. Maps with the most up-to-date information about the location of German guns were marked in red. Once the course was determined, only the pilot and navigator knew exactly where the plane was going.

Organizing the packing and production of supplies to be dropped from the plane took place fifty miles from Harrington. Tucked deep in a wooded area not obvious from the sky nor accessible by train, over three hundred men worked at "Area H," a special operations supply station that never turned off the lights. Buildings that housed explosives were built away from the main part of the camp and were reinforced with brick walls in case of an unexpected explosion. Barbed wire fences and guard dogs provided security. Inside the sheet metal buildings, the men worked to prepare cargo for the Carpetbagger missions. Even though the drops were made a mere three hundred feet from the earth, dropping explosive materials motivated the mission planners to come up with a safe way to pack the potentially deadly cargo. Cylinder shaped containers were constructed with a shock-absorbing buffer on one end. Partitions divided the insides of the containers to separate different items. These containers could weigh up to three hundred pounds. The Liberator had room for up to a dozen of these canisters. Another type of container, a pannier, resembled a woven basket. Stuffed with corrugated paper, it would carry fragile items like radio sets. Small parachutes were hand sewn on the grounds of the supply station to be attached to every canister and basket dropped from the plane. Not surprisingly, the items most requested by the Resistance fighters were guns and ammunition. Many other things used to fight a guerilla war were supplied as well, including gasoline, blood plasma, food, knifes, and grenades. Great care was taken to make all the items appear to have originated in France. English trademarks were replaced with French ones and any clothing sent was of the style worn by French men and women.

Once the airplane was loaded with supplies, the crew was transported by truck to their plane. If spies were dropped on a mission, they were brought to the plane just before takeoff. For every Carpetbagger mission, the forces on the ground were given a special code from London that would serve as the confirming signal of the drop spot. These messages were broadcast to occupied Europe on BBC Radio in code. The phrases, "Uncle Jean has two shillings in his pocket," or "The beet does not improve the salad," would inform an underground radio operator that a plane would be flying that night and where the drop would occur.

"We were given the coordinates where to drop. Sometimes we wouldn't see a thing 'til all of a sudden we'd see holes in the ground and there'd be fire in 'em. The holes were maybe three feet deep with a cover over 'em to hide the fire until they heard our airplane coming. Oh, hell yes, our plane would have been loud. Usually by that time we'd have to pull away and get a long run at it because a lot of time we'd be right over the drop before we'd see them. So, we'd have to go around, back off, load the gear, and slow down. And all you're thinking is how you want to get the hell out of there. We were afraid someone would pick us up and shoot us down with a damn rifle at that altitude. They could shoot the engine or

shoot the inside of the plane. It was just a tin deal, aluminum. That was a critical moment from the time the navigator spotted the light. He was the one who could usually see it, or the bombardier would be looking out the nose of the plane and would see the signal. He would talk to the pilot and tell him what he was seeing. The pilot would know the code. Then we would drop on that light. We'd drop out the canisters and guys on the ground would come out and load 'em into carts, wagons. We dropped everything. We didn't see a lot of what we dropped. It was probably mostly ammunition, small arms, money. The supplies were in a container, big round tube like a bomb. Drop it out the bomb bay door."

The drops of cargo and spies were made at less than 600 feet from the ground. The plane was slowed to a speed of around 130 miles per hour, barely fast enough to prevent stalling. *"We had to go full RPM with the flaps and gear down, just like we were comin' in for a landing."* These low drops greatly endangered the crew but helped protect fragile cargo from breaking and eased the already difficult jump for the spies. The low speed was necessary to prevent the parachutes from bursting.

After a drop was made, the Carpetbagger crew would continue to fly deeper into Nazi-occupied territory. This decoy move was to confuse the Germans of the actual target. Sometimes the crew would dump pamphlets to lead the enemy to think that the purpose of the mission was to fight with propaganda. The missions typically were expected to take between five and eight hours. Immediately upon return of the airplane to Harrington, the crew met in the base's interrogation room. Sitting at a picnic table supplied with aspirin, sleeping pills, water, coffee, and a bottle of whiskey, the crew was questioned about every aspect of the mission. They were asked if they located the drop spot and if the signal matched the pre-arranged code. They gave detailed reports about weather conditions, looking for the rate of accuracy of the forecasts. Weather conditions would also have a great deal of influence over where the drops ultimately landed. They were asked if they saw any ground fire or if they were spotted by search lights. Tail gunner Phillips, who had the best opportunity to see, was quizzed regarding what he observed happened to the cargo and spies after they were dropped. Any report of gunfire from the enemy on the flight to and from the drop zone was of great interest. This information helped update maps of enemy artillery locations. After interrogation, the crew was trucked to the mess hall where a cook was waiting to serve them a meal considered much better than standard military food at the time. *"We had fresh eggs, bacon, and pancakes."* With full stomachs, the crew headed off to sleep. The crew might be called for another mission the next day. If the weather was bad, it could be several days before they took to the air again. *"Damn right it felt good to be back."*

The procedural description of Operation Carpetbagger is how things were designed to work on paper. In reality, getting the spies and their cargo to the secret drop spots would prove much trickier.

CHAPTER 8
The Work Begins

"...the requirements for a military aviator call for more concentrated physical and mental ability in the individual than has ever been necessary in any calling before."

Brigadier General William "Billy" Mitchell

Though his mother had always teased Royce to fly *"low and slow,"* in reality, this is the most dangerous way to fly. Low altitudes at near stalling speed on their twenty-eight-ton airplane was exactly the kind of flying required of the Carpetbaggers. And just like the bootlegging operations that ran under cover of darkness, so did the Carpetbaggers. Their mission training had taught them how to fly in the daytime, avoiding enemy fire. Now, instead of dropping bombs, they were going to be flying at night dropping spies and the supplies they and others on the ground needed for their hit-and-run warfare. The Borden crew needed a completely different type of training for their assignment.

"On our first mission in England, we flew across the Channel to France. We took off from another airfield, not our base in Harrington. They gave us a regular bomber that was used for training. It was my job as engineer to make sure all the systems were working. We took off at night and went over the Channel. It was an orientation flight to experience flying by ourselves at night. A learning flight is what it amounted to. Borden said to test fire the guns as we crossed the Channel. I climbed into the top turret to fire my guns and the guns had not been put back correctly in the holder. Those fifty-caliber machine guns fell into pieces onto the floor of the airplane. There's a little pin press on the side that loosens the back plate. When I pulled it, the back plate came off and the whole guts of the machine guns came out. It was night so I had to put 'em together without any light. In gunnery school we had to pass a test on machine guns where we had to be able to put 'em

back together in so many minutes with gloves on, blind-folded. I knew I had to set the barrel head where it won't swell up or misfire. You have so many clicks on the barrel to make it work. I had to replace the two guns in the turret. There were notches that connected the machine gun barrel into the body of the gun. It would get hot and freeze up if you didn't have the clicks right on the machine gun. My training did come in good! I didn't have to see anything, I just knew the way everything should fit. Yes, I fixed the guns and they fired."

When the Carpetbagger missions first began, experienced combat crews were recruited for these difficult solo night flights. Their combat experience, along with an additional month of training, helped prepare them for the unique flying conditions they would face. The Borden crew had arrived at Harrington during the second phase of the operation. In the several months before their arrival, up to forty airplanes a night were assigned secret drop targets. The push had been to supply Resistance forces in France prior to D-Day. The Borden crew arrived after the invasion. By September of 1944, German presence in France was reduced to small groups in fortified enclaves. The Carpetbagger missions then spread to surrounding countries: Norway, Denmark, Holland, Belgium, and even Germany itself. More spies were dropped than in earlier missions, providing critical support until the end of the War. The Borden crew and others who found themselves in the second phase of the Carpetbagger mission had yet another challenge thrown at them. They did not have the luxury of a month of training before their missions began. In fact, just weeks after their arrival at Station 179, the Borden Crew was one of several crews given the daylight assignment of delivering gas to stranded ground tanks being led by one of the most successful field commanders in U.S. history—General George Smith Patton, Jr.

After the Battle of Normandy, General Patton led his ground troops in their armored tanks across Europe. They advanced at so fast a pace that supply systems could not keep pace. It became clear that fuel would have to be brought in by air. Carpetbagger crews were called in for help. Once again, their Liberators had to be modified. This time the airplanes had tanks installed that could carry over thirteen hundred gallons of fuel. The Borden Crew's destination would be France. For ten dangerous days in September of 1944, crude landing strips crumbled under the weight of the planes loaded with as much gas as they could hold. By the end of this operation, nearly a million gallons of fuel would be transported to Patton's tanks.

"Five of our missions were gas hauls. We didn't have the radio operator or the dispatcher on these missions. Overnight, Patton had stalled outside of Belgium. He'd run out of gas. So they woke me, the pilot, co-pilot, navigator, and tail gunner up. It was just a five-man crew for this job. Patton was really goin' for the Germans. Bomb groups were helping as well. We landed on a bombed-out air strip put together to get those gas planes in there. They'd filled the bomb holes with rocks. The wheels of the plane would settle into the rock and fire would fly! The tail would hit the ground and we'd see sparks. Not a very smooth landing. We would line our planes up, head to tail, and wait for the guys to pump out the gas. There would be six or eight airplanes in line. Our tail gunner, Phillips, would be in his turret the whole time, guarding against enemy fire. The guys on the ground would attach a hose to the plane to pump the

fuel into a pipeline that went straight to Patton's supply line. They would pump our wing tanks too and leave us just enough fuel to get back across the Channel."

Though the war had clearly turned in favor of the Allies at this point, German forces continued to fight aggressively. German fighter pilots who flew under cover of darkness, "Night Fighters," remained a threat. *"We were lined up on the airfield after they had pumped out our gas. There were half-a-dozen planes there and it was getting dark. There was always a concern about Night Fighters. So, they turned the lights off and said, 'No more flights tonight.' We were the only night-flyers there. The other guys were bombers who only flew in daylight. Borden told 'em to call London and tell them who we are and that we wanted to take off! Because we had experience flying at night, they gave us clearance out of London and we pulled out of the row and took off."* Roaring with laughter while remembering this takeoff, Royce continued, *"You could sit on the top of the plane there, out through the top hatch. I was sittin' up there wavin' to the other guys on the ground. We were going home, see. The other crews were gonna' have to spend the night there, stay with their plane, sleep under the wings. That was pretty cocky of me. We thought we were tough shit. We did feel pretty proud when they let us go. We flew at night all the time. That was our specialty."*

The Borden Crew had confidence in their ability to fly at night, but they did not take for granted the real threat of the German Night Fighters. American bombers flew by day, the Royal Air Force dropped bombs at night. Germany modified several of their airplanes to strike at night. These heavily armed, fast-moving planes were equipped with radar that allowed them to target unsuspecting planes and attack without warning. *"Once in a while, on the way back from a mission, we'd lose one of our planes. A Night Fighter would sneak under the airplane and attack. We were always aware of them when we would come in for our final approach. The Night Fighter could get under our radar then and could shoot the plane down when landing. We had to be aware of that."*

As the Borden crew experienced firsthand, the evasive maneuvers used to get away from these deadly planes could potentially be as dangerous as the Night Fighters. *"I believe we were flying somewhere around Holland, coming home from a drop. Our radar picked up a Night Fighter. Radar was just in the early stages then. The radar would only go straight out the back of the plane in a cone shape. There was a lighting system at the back of the plane in the tail gunner's turret. The green light was on all the time; that meant the radar was working. A yellow light meant there was a plane in the range of the cone. If the red light came on it meant there was a plane right on us and then the tail gunner would press a button launching a weapon. We couldn't tell if we hit anything unless the plane following us went down. We picked up a Night Fighter in our cone. He hadn't hit us. In order to get away from him, we ducked into a cloud. Duckin' into clouds to hide was something we normally did. But this cloud was a storm cloud, a cumulonimbus cloud. The wind inside that cloud was going up and down. When Borden ducked us into that cloud it threw us up to the top and we flipped. We had been tossed upside down in the bomber. It was kind of like flying in a loop where you don't fall against the seat belt because of centrifugal force. When we came down from bein' flipped, damn it was nasty in that plane. Some of the* *things in the plane got loose and were falling around. We noticed that the gyro had been tumbled. Our pilot flew us out of that son-of-a-bitch cloud and we flew back to base. He controlled the plane and brought us home. When we landed and they checked the plane it was clear we had been up-side down. That is not good in a bomber. That was **real** bad. While we were in the thick of it, there was nothing I could do. I just had to hold on at that point. We were in the storm cloud maybe five minutes. You don't have time to think about dying. You're thinking, 'What the hell's going on?' That was one of the times I felt we were really in danger."*

In addition to threats from the air, enemy ground fire was also a danger. Though the Allies made a concerted effort to track the location of enemy ground artillery, anytime the airplane was flying there was the possibility of attack. *"We'd go over the coast, the English Channel. We learned to avoid Night Fighters there by getting right on deck. If we had something on our tail, we'd drop so low, to almost a spray. Maybe to fifty, a hundred feet. They couldn't sneak under us then. We would also dive down low to get below radar. So we'd enter the Channel at maybe five thousand feet, pick up extra speed, maybe get to two hundred and ten miles per hour. Then we'd pull up to go over the coast, the bank there. The Germans on the ground would still have the covers on their guns. They had a lot of small caliber guns, forty, fifty caliber. We'd be on 'em before they could run to their guns. We'd see 'em trying to get the covers off. But by the time they did, we'd be gone. That was the idea of surprise. It was in this area that we had the most fire. The Germans had search lights along the coastline that would sweep the sky. The lights were lined up to make a continuous sweep, one light after another. The light was so bright in the airplane you could read a newspaper by it. We would have to take evasive action to get away from that."*

The Carpetbagger crews had earned the right to be proud of their skills. Even if they were free from enemy fire in the air or on the ground, night flying at low altitudes was dangerous, a fact not missed by Royce. *"Night flying was a serious deal. Low, slow flying is extremely dangerous. And there were mountains all around us. That was the biggest danger for us. That was the reason for most of our losses."* The mountainous areas of south central and eastern France, areas that often contained drop sites, could prove deadly to huge aircraft maneuvering in the dark. *"One of the other times I felt we were really in danger was when we were flying down in the mountains in France. We had found our drop site and were headin' home. All of a sudden our navigator Barton says, 'Pull up, pull up!' Borden hit the throttles forward and we just damn near ran into a mountain. He sheared off to the left there. We skirted over that son-of-a-bitch. That was close. Radar did not go out in the front of the plane at that point. It was very primitive. The navigator saved our ass. It was at night, of course. That was the scariest deal. We almost got leaves from trees caught on the plane, we were so low."* The official training protocol for the B-24 emphasizes the need to calculate response times for maneuvering the plane. The Liberator had a reputation among pilots for being sluggish. For the Borden Crew headed straight into a mountain, the airplane and pilot beat the odds and somehow worked together to prevent a disaster.

Sometimes there were no explanations for why things went deadly wrong. *"We were comin' home after a mission and fog came rollin' in. We had to make a landing in an emergency airfield in England so we could wait for the fog to burn off. That night we got a poker game goin' and the engineer on another crew had taken most of our money. The next morning they served us mutton and tomatoes for breakfast. It was ridiculous. I couldn't eat it. The engineer who'd won our money was on the crew that took off right before we did. We were lined up behind them, getting ready to take off immediately after their plane. As they were taking off, they crashed right into a damned tree. It just wiped 'em out, all of them. I don't know for sure what happened to the plane. The plane might have lost power. We had to fly over that crash site. Of course it was just another plane crash. It was nothing new. We'd seen them before. No question about it that all the guys on the crew died. We were already at the end of the runway. We had to continue our take off."*

Though Royce is hesitant about saying it, the Borden Crew quickly developed a reputation as a team that could accomplish a job other crews could not. *"There was a guy who'd been dropped out of a British Mosquito bomber into Holland. Holland was flooded at the time and when he'd dropped, his chute burst and he broke his leg when he landed. He hadn't been heard from for a long time. He did get a message out that he needed money and ammunition. Since the British had dropped him, they sent a couple of their crews in to look for him. They couldn't find him. This guy needed money, that was the big thing. All his stuff had fallen into the water. We went out lookin' for his code. We did find it. Our navigator was just fantastic. That was one of the toughest, hard to find. The location was just an 'X' out there in the middle of the wilderness. He had a flashlight, just a one-man operation. We dropped a canister to him. We didn't know for sure what was in it, but I'm certain it had money inside. We all felt pretty cocky about locating him."*

The Carpetbaggers took risks with their airplanes no other Liberator crews did. They flew in weather conditions that would ground other operations. But the crews involved in these special missions were not the only brave fighters. Young men and women who were trained to be spies flew on many of the Borden crew's missions, literally throwing themselves onto land controlled by the Nazis.

CHAPTER 9
"Churchill's Secret Army"

The spies that climbed into the Liberators knew the dangers facing them. One of four would perish on their secret assignments. The Carpetbaggers dropped over five hundred agents behind enemy lines. *"Dropping spies, that was the interesting part about our missions. There were three different kinds of people that we dropped. One was individual spies. Another group was saboteurs. They were the guys who would blow stuff up. They would usually be a couple or more working together. The other group was Jed Teams. The Jed Teams were made of three people. We used them at the end of the war quite a* *bit. They would go in there and manage one of these underground groups."* The Jed Teams were highly trained men: two officers and one enlisted man. Efforts were made to place one officer on the mission who was a native from the occupied country. Their duties were to equip and train Resistance fighters and to lead the groups in conducting special operations against the Germans.

All the men and women transported by the Carpetbaggers had undergone extensive training for the dangerous work they would do behind enemy lines. An initial interview process looked for candidates that were intelligent, well-educated, coolheaded, and loyal. There were several levels of training that both men and women would complete together. For British agents, their education began with a two-to-three-week training where they learned basic map reading, how to shoot pistols and submachine guns, and were required to get physically fit. If they passed this level, the future agents were sent to a remote area off the western coast of Scotland for paramilitary training. Only one narrow road led into this "no-go" area where the training agenda included teaching unarmed combat techniques. They learned to kill silently by creeping up behind an enemy and slicing the throat. The students learned how to explode trains and bridges. They practiced ambushing and storming a house. If they passed this level, the candidates were sent to "finishing school." While staying at one of a dozen country houses around Beaulieu Manor in the New Forest of southeastern England, the new spies were taught how to survive in Nazi-occupied territory. Blackmail, burglary, and forgery were part of the curriculum. The spies-in-training learned how to react if suddenly questioned by a member of the German Army or Gestapo. They were coached to be inconspicuous by giving up their English habits and acting more French. Seemingly minor traits such as sipping a soup spoon from the side or looking right first instead of left when crossing the street could blow their cover. The final stage of the training occurred at Ringway, Scotland. Just like dispatcher Keishnick, every spy had to learn to jump from an airplane. If they passed the training, they were instructed to write their wills and await their assignment.

"It was a rule that we were not to talk to the spies. A lot of them didn't speak English anyway.

They were trained for months: the way to eat, the language, how to wear their hair. They didn't want to speak any language except the one they would be using in the country they were goin' in. A lot of the women were French, some were German, some American. They all were volunteers." The agents were delivered to the Carpetbagger base about four hours before their takeoff. They were immediately taken to a dressing hut where they put on a loose-fitting jumpsuit. Searched for any item that could disclose secret information, the spies were given guns, knives, a compass, money, a folding shovel to bury their parachute, and any other items specific to their mission. The men also carried a gold watch, the women a gold makeup compact, to be used to barter with or bribe. A final mission briefing that included disbursement of pills, some lethal, was carried out. After the crew was in their Liberator, the spies were taken by car to the waiting airplane.

"When we were briefed about our assignment, we were told about how important it was. We were told how these people (the spies) operated. This one guy came back and told us about what was goin' on. He'd been an agent. We were to supply for the

underground in France, especially. There were cells all over Europe, mainly in France, Belgium, and Holland. When they boarded the airplane, the spies would have a package with them with supplies. Some of them traveled pretty damn light, but some of them had leg bags that dropped down ten to fifteen feet below when they jumped. The bags were tied to their leg, stayed with them when they dropped. They had ammo in them, of course. When we got near the drop, the spies would move to the Joe Hole. They would sit down and put their feet in that hole. Keishnick would feel some resistance at times when it was time for them to jump out. But once they get their feet in the hole and he's got 'em by their back straps and his knees are in their backs, he just kicks 'em out!"

By the time Operation Carpetbagger began, women were being recruited to serve as agents. Despite the provision of the Geneva Convention that prohibited women from engaging in combat duties, the SOE, with the endorsement of Winston Churchill, decided women could bring unique skills to espionage. Women could more easily blend in behind enemy lines. They were not obvious combatants, nor were they being rounded up as men were for forced labor. Traveling on trains or riding on bikes with explosives hidden in their bags did not arouse as much suspicion. Despite these advantages, less than four dozen female agents were dropped into occupied France. The Borden crew transported more than a handful.

"We were given the coordinates where to drop a young girl spy. The word was that her family had been killed by Germans. We dropped her in the Pyrenees Mountains. We were close to Switzerland. Switzerland had lights on the border with Germany. We could use those lights to help us find an IP (initial point). It looked crazy to see lights there and then France blacked out. We could see the border, so we'd know to turn around there and head to the Alps. There were two ranges in there, the Pyrenees and the Alps. That was her drop. That girl bailed out in the damn wilderness by herself. We dropped her right where she was supposed to be dropped. She was going to mingle with the German soldiers. Spy on them. She would have a radio to get back as a way of contacting London."

The contributions of female spies have only recently been properly recognized. After the War, government officials in Great Britain were hesitant to discuss the accomplishments of female spies for fear of admitting the danger in which they were placed. Civilian medals were offered but were seen by the women as an insult as they did not recognize their contributions. Their brave accomplishments cannot be overlooked. Of the thirty-nine female agents dropped into France, fifteen were executed.

The very nature of the work the Borden Crew did makes it difficult to know precisely who they were transporting, let alone other details of the spy's mission. *"When the crew got in the airplane, the only ones who knew where we were goin' was the pilot and the navigator. We were told not to talk to the spies. We were there to do our particular job and that was it."* There was, however, one mission recalled by Royce that was much different than the usual spy drop.

"Pierre Laval, the Prime Minister of France, had turned the French government over to the Germans. We had been sent to Lyon, France—flew into an airport there. Laval had a four-story house there on

a hillside outside of Lyon. It was said that he was sitting in a chair by his big fireplace during the invasion. And when the invasion got going, he supposedly got up and stretched and said, 'It's time for me to go.' When we were in Lyon, we were in this house. I sat in that chair. They were keeping spies there. We were there for a few days while waiting for a sixteen-year-old German kid to be debriefed. He was a double-agent and we went there to pick him up. Nobody else would drop him. The British wouldn't drop him. That's why I think they kind of singled us (the Borden Crew) out. We agreed to drop him. This kid had his own gang in Germany. He had been a German agent. He'd been caught and we brainwashed him and we was gonna take him back as our guy and drop him with his team inside of Germany there."

It appears there was a great deal of concern about whether the young German boy had really decided to fight for the Allies. Many precautions were taken when dealing with the hopefully former teenage-Nazi. *"When they brought him out to the airplane, we had the engines runnin'. The black curtains were drawn. A chauffeur brought this guy out to the plane in an* old tourin' car. He had four or five beautiful girls in the car with him. I don't know who they were, but they were all over him. Kissing and rubbin' all over him. Two of them got into the airplane with him. They brought him through a back access panel—not the usual way for spies—through the Joe Hole. They were with him every minute, distracting his thoughts so he couldn't remember a lot about where he came from and what we were doing. They didn't want him to give his situation away cause he was going to be a double-agent. I guess the concern was that he would become a triple agent! He was a different deal. The Allies took a chance that he would do stuff for us back in Germany."

The tension during the drop of the young, blonde-headed boy from Germany was greater than normal missions. "I didn't talk with the boy, of course. During the flight I was checking all over the airplane. Keishnick was the one who talked to him in German. The boy knew he was close to the target area when Keishnick opened the Joe Hole. He told Keishnick where we were. He knew exactly because we were taking him home, see. That kid was smart. He had been searched; he wasn't supposed to have a gun.

There was a fear that this kid would try and sabotage our airplane, cut the cables or something, and bail out. People were afraid of him. Keishnick kept his eye on him the entire time. We wasn't supposed to bring him back. I remember that if he didn't jump, we were just supposed to put him out without a chute. I know that sounds bad, but shit, that's nothing. Just before the kid jumped, he did pull out a little automatic from his coveralls. Keishnick was supposed to shoot him if the kid had a gun. But Keishnick had been talking to the kid and Keishnick had his gun ready. The kid didn't make a big deal out of pulling his gun out. He just exposed it, put a round in the chamber just before he jumped. Keishnick made the judgment call that the kid wanted to be ready to protect himself when he hit the ground. It was the right call. We dropped the kid and came back home."

.

CHAPTER 10
Lost and Found

Like the other crews living at Station 179, the lives of the Borden Crew, when they were not in the air, were pleasantly mundane. As a child, Royce had experienced hunger firsthand. He knew what it felt like to be unsure where he would lay his head at night. So, despite the danger the crew faced on their missions, the security of everyday life on the base was comforting to Royce.

"Our crew liked to play cards: poker, hearts, gin rummy. We played for money, no high stakes, just small amounts. There really wasn't a lot to do when we weren't flyin'. I'd read some. Our crew would meet every day even if we weren't flying. We had a

mess hall. We'd ride bicycles there from our Quonset Huts. We'd try and sneak marmalade back to our hut. Orange marmalade was a new thing; nasty shit, it was full of seeds. We liked grape. The guy working in the mess hall at night would slip us out a case— came in half-gallon cans. We could get good, fresh bread in the mail room. The local woman made it. We had peanut butter—would make sandwiches. One night the Red Cross USO threw us a party. There was dancin' and everything. I won an apple pie. We had to leave the party that night to go to work. It was a tremendous way to live. It was just fun. I guess it was a good place for an adrenaline junkie."

Though parts of Royce's life on base were nicer than anything he had known previously, there were constant reminders that he and the other men were at war. *"After D-Day, the Allies were still flyin' a lot of bomb missions. U.S. bombers would run during the day, but the British bombers flew at night. The British had a beacon out behind our Quonset area. That's where the British planes would form up, on that beacon. They'd take off, climb up, and then gather up. I don't know how they didn't run into each other. I never figured that out. I couldn't believe it.*

Shit yeah, you could hear them from our hut. There would be a swarm, fifty or sixty airplanes, all climbing to get their altitude, meeting at a gathering point in the sky."

Though preoccupied with the work required by the missions, Royce and his crewmates were aware of the bigger picture of what was happening during the War. *"We knew about the concentration camps. We had been warned about not getting caught if we had to bail out of our plane. We were not protected by the Geneva Convention, and if they caught us, they would give us the same treatment they gave the spies. That was one thing about our job that wasn't exactly easy. Supposedly the interrogation for us was a little extra. We knew about supplyin' the underground. We would have information about where we dropped people off. It was suggested to us that we not give up information, especially the people on the crew who knew the exact locations of the drops. The guys who knew what was goin' on had cyanide tablets to take. You didn't want to get caught. There was a lot of talk about torture. Course we also had the other end of it. If we got shot down or crashed, why the underground would get us out of there, take care of us, see."*

As the Borden Crew had seen firsthand many times, a crash often meant the death of fellow airmen. *"My crew never got hurt. I don't know why we didn't, just luck. I've thought about that lots of times. Why us?"* Royce was forced to ask himself this question about a pilot he had worked with and grew to respect while they were both in training with their new crews in Colorado. Royce was surprised to learn that this pilot, Second Lieutenant Lawrence Berkhoff, had also been assigned to the Carpetbagger mission. *"When we were assembling as combat crews at Peterson Field, Colorado, I flew extra training missions with a pilot by the name of Berkhoff. I filled in for his flight engineer who was sick. I flew with him at least a couple of times to keep him and his crew up. It was quite a coincidence that we both ended up as Carpetbaggers."*

As enlisted man Fulmer would learn, a shared history between himself and Officer Berkhoff did not justify casual conversation. *"One day I was down by the water well on my bicycle. I saw Berkhoff there and I didn't salute. Instead I said, 'Hi, Berkee!' No one was around when I said this. It was a private situation. Berkhoff stopped me and chewed my ass for not saluting him! So of course, I saluted him. He got lost the next week. The whole crew got lost. Never did see him again."*

If a crew took off for a mission and did not return, it was more than likely that the men on base would not learn the fate of the missing crew. Not returning could mean the airmen had bailed out and escaped with the help of the underground. It could have meant capture, or it could have meant death. This information, impossible for the men of Station 179 to discover during the War, is readily available today.

The Berkhoff Crew arrived at Harrington the same time as the Borden Crew, August of 1944. When Berkhoff's men flew on September 8th, they had only been on one observer mission. The September mission was their first Carpetbagger drop. Shortly after their late-night takeoff, a long flame was seen coming out the exhaust. After flying several circles, the flames disappeared. With the large flame gone, the decision was made to head on to the target. But the constant glow from the plane made it a target for Night Fighters so Berkhoff turned back. On the return home, Berkhoff's B-24 lost two engines on the same side of the plane. The airplane began to rapidly fall from the sky. Berkhoff, the leader of the crew, ordered his men to bail out. The plane was at 3,300 feet. His flight engineer, Alphonse Rinz, stayed on the plane long enough to experience the plane twisting out of Berkhoff's control. The plane was headed toward an English village. At 1,000 feet, flight engineer Rinze yelled at Berkhoff to bail with him but Burkhoff stayed at the helm, fighting with the controls to crash the plane away from the village. Unknown to Berkhoff, the village in the path of the descending Liberator was Lambourn. Located in the southeastern part of Berkshire County, England, gold bracelets dating back to 1200 B.C. have been found here. The beloved author JRR Tolkien lived near this village. All Berkhoff knew as he stayed with his plane was that the mission now was to avoid the village. The plane went into a spiral and dove straight into the ground in a field beside Folly Road, just a couple hundred yards from Lambourn. Rinze saw the crash from the air as he had not yet landed from his jump. The other crew members landed their jumps safely, suffering only minor injuries. Pilot Lawrence Berkhoff, a native of

Bronx County, New York, was twenty years old when he died in a field just outside Lambourn.

For those of us that are old enough, we remember when research required the physical act of going to a library and using paper indexes to look for answers to our queries. Those too young for this memory may perhaps take for granted the ease of gathering a quick answer to most any question. For a ninety-year-old Royce who had never looked at a computer screen prior to this project, witnessing internet searches for the first time was *"great, stupendous!"*

Prior to writing his memoir, Royce had no idea what had happened to Berkhoff. Royce's recollection of him occurred while thinking about his training experiences and things that happened to him while living on base. Royce knew he had stepped out of line when he didn't salute Berkhoff, but at the same time, his nearly seventy-year-old memory still harbored irritation at being scolded by a young officer with whom Royce had worked. *"I felt bad about him chastising me. I had flown with him in training missions in Colorado when his flight engineer was sick. I helped to keep his crew up to a training level."* The new knowledge of Berkhoff's heroism instantly changed his feelings toward the fallen airman. *"Well, I'm gonna have to change my mind about him, I guess."*

.

CHAPTER 11
Headin' Home

After thirty missions, no one on the Borden Crew had suffered a serious injury. Their Liberator had only a few scrapes from German bullets. Yet the crew had witnessed the deaths of fellow Airmen firsthand. They also were left wondering what happened to their colleagues whose cots remained empty after a mission. The crews could only imagine the fate of the young men and women they dropped in the night. The accomplishments of the Resistance fighters would come to light after the war. But one thing that was obvious to the men on the Borden airplane was the technological success of the Germans when it came to creating a weapon that could reach farther and faster than any weapon ever used in war.

"The night we got the most action was the night we saw a V-2 bomb come right up by our airplane. We were on our way home from a drop, flying about 10,000 feet up. The rocket was red hot, about the size of a box car. That damned thing just kept goin' higher and higher in the sky." The Borden crew had nearly run into the first object to enter outer space. Developed by Wernher von Braun, this rocket that could fly for two hundred miles at a speed of over 3,000 miles an hour, would hit Britain with devastating force, killing and injuring almost 9,000 people living on the Island. *"It was a long-range deal the Germans were firing right into London."* The first rocket to hit England was launched on September 8, 1944. That was a busy week for the Borden crew. They flew four missions from the 10th of September to the 17th. Seventy years later, the memory of seeing that rocket remained strong in tail gunner Phillips, the first man to spot the red glow, "It was something to see! I said, 'Look at that thing coming through the sky there!' Man, it was moving." When the crew arrived home from the mission, Phillips made the report of

the rocket at the de-briefing. Royce recalls the officers were *"very anxious to find out all the details. We sat down at the table, told them everything we saw. Then they gave us a couple a shots of whiskey."*

The impression that glowing fireball made on Pilot Borden shaped the course of his career. After the war, he entered Yale Law School. But before beginning his legal studies, Borden wrote a book that was inspired by what he saw from his Liberator. The foreword to *There Will Be No Time, The Revolution in Strategy*, tells in Borden's own words the significance of that night:

"The emotional impetus for this book came from a German V-2 rocket. One night in November 1944, I was flying a Liberator bomber back to England after a mission to Holland. Only the fluorescent instrument panel relieved the darkness on our flight deck, the ship guided itself on auto-pilot, and we were about to cross the British coast in routine fashion. Suddenly the cockpit lit up with crimson glare. I thought the flash must have come from a gasoline explosion in the plane, but looking above we glimpsed the fiery streak of a V-2 headed for London. It resembled a meteor, streaming red sparks and whizzing past us as though the aircraft were motionless. Our Liberator, whose speed had once seemed fairly impressive, now appeared as a primitive horse-drawn buggy. We had spent nearly two hours returning from Holland, and it would be another half-hour until we touched down at base. The V-2 left Holland some four minutes before overtaking us, and it struck London before the navigator even had time to make a note of the incident in his flight log. To realize intellectually that fourteen-ton missiles can travel four or five times the speed of sound is one thing, and to experience the dazzling impact of such speed upon the senses is quite another. Along with every other man aboard our Liberator who glanced up fast enough to catch an impression of the V-2, I became convinced that it was only a matter of time until rockets would expose the United States to direct, transoceanic attack. Hence this effort to think straight about the strategic implications of the new weapons."

After the completion of their thirty missions, Royce never talked to Borden again. The two men who had worked so well together had discussed continuing their partnership, volunteering to fly to China. *"Borden asked me if I'd like to go with him to China. Get a crew together and go. We would have dropped security personnel around the prison camps there, tryin' to get our guys in there to help the ones that were captured. There was concern the prisoners in the camps were gonna be killed. We wanted to give them some backup. I told Borden yes; I told him I would go. I wanted to go. But at that point, the war was basically over. Everybody came back home then."*

Borden would write his book, graduate from law school, and begin his legal career working for the Justice Department. Eventually he would become the Executive Director of the Joint Atomic Energy Committee. Some of his views concerning nuclear strategy were seen as radical. The main point of his book was that unless the U.S. and the Soviet Union merged their two governments, an event he acknowledged was extremely unlikely, nuclear war between the two sovereigns was inevitable. His beliefs were nothing if not sincerely held. In a letter to President Truman that had been drafted by Borden on behalf of the chairman of the Joint Committee on Atomic Energy, Borden pushed for a significant expansion of the United States' nuclear arsenal, arguing, "If we let Russia get the super first, catastrophe becomes all but certain—whereas, if we get it first, there exists a chance for saving ourselves." Borden's strongly-held opinions on the nuclear arms race extended to atomic scientists. In the fall of 1953, Borden wrote a letter to FBI Director J. Edgar Hoover expressing his conclusion that Robert Oppenheimer was an agent for the Soviet Union. It was this controversial letter and congressional testimony that would follow that were instrumental in branding Oppenheimer a spy.

For Royce, the end of the war meant the return to South Carolina. *"What happened after our last mission? I didn't do a big handstand or anything. No party. Everybody just flew the coop—heading home. We didn't know it would be the last mission before we flew it. We just came home. I came back on the Queen Mary. My bunk was three decks down. The cots were three levels. Crowded as shit down there. There was* a stink. I believe it took us fourteen days to get back. We were still at war, so they were zig-zaggin' the boat on the way back. They'd run the ship one way for so many minutes then turn it back and forth. There was some concern about the safety of the trip. Most of the time I had a crap game goin'. I didn't play, I ran it. I got a percentage of the winnings depending on the size of the pot. Think I won $2,500, though a thousand of it was in Canadian money, ninety cents on the dollar. Of course, you would shoot that money first. Yeah, I did pretty damn well on my gambling deal. I'd been playin' since I was a teen. I always had a pair of dice with me. We'd turn a bench upside down, put a blanket over it. You hold the blanket tight and don't bump your dice on the board. You just roll the damn thing out on the blanket. You could roll a lot of good stuff like that, winning points. If you stack the dice just right and you throw 'em, bang 'em against something, then you're not controlling the dice. It's skill. Everyone had the same opportunity. You could find out pretty easily that if you put a six on the top of a one and then shoot them out there then you'll get a seven or eleven. Everybody was doing the same thing."

Royce didn't tell anyone that his tour was over, "*I just went home.*" After the Queen Mary docked in New York City, Royce made his way south to be discharged from the Service. "*They put us on a train headed to Florida. We didn't do anything there. We were just waiting to get out of there.*" Though the plan with Borden had not worked out, he was not ready to leave the service. "*When I came back to the States, they were looking for tail gunners on B-29s. In fact, they were beggin' for combat crew members to fly tail gunner on this plane. It was a hell of a bad deal, but I volunteered for this. I was stupid, but now I see how luck handled it. I was finishing up my gunnery school for the B-29 in Shreveport, Louisiana. That's where I was when we dropped the bombs. I was all ready to go and then the damn war was over. When I heard the news, I was back in Charleston. I was on King Street. Bells were ringing. I was relieved. I tell ya, that was a pretty fun night.*"

With the war over, Royce's plans to be a gunner in the South Pacific ended. Instead, he returned to his mother's boarding house on Main Street in Columbia, South Carolina.

CHAPTER 12
Figuring Things Out

At the age of twenty-two, Royce had flown thirty combat missions, had spent thousands of hours in the air, and knew every detail about the mechanics of a state-of-the-art airplane. Yet he was missing one thing he was determined to have: a high school diploma.

"I had all of that war experience, but I still went back to high school. The girls, they went crazy when I went in there. I was a hero as far as they were concerned. I wore my leather bomber jacket. The girls, they just hollered. I got all kinds of preferential treatment. The principal, an ex-Army major from the First War, called me into his office and told me he

knew how it was gonna be for me to come back to school. He knew it would be strange for me to be with a bunch of kids. He told me if I needed to take a smoke break, I could walk across the street to the drug store, but of course I didn't smoke. Because of my age they gave me a special permit to play football. I played one game. I did it to ride the bus." After a year of studies, Royce graduated from Brooklyn-Cayce High School. *"There's a war memorial there. My name's on a brick because I served."*

Though he had spent many challenging hours in the air, Royce had never held the controls of a plane in his own hands. Determined to get his pilot's license, Royce enrolled in the training program at the Hawthorne Flying Service in Columbia while he was still attending high school. *"It was easy for me to learn how to fly. My instructor was a woman. She was picky. She got pissed at me because I was kind of loose. I was nonchalant. I started flyin' solo after I'd been there a couple of weeks. My second day I took a buddy on a ride, Harry Dominick. He'd parked his car by the side of the road and I taxied over to him. He jumped in the plane, ducked down in the back to hide, and we took off. I don't know if he was brave or stupid. Maybe a little of both. He trusted me. He thought I could do anything."*

Royce's confidence did not go unnoticed by the man who owned and operated the flight school. Beverly Howard, "Bevo," had a lot of experience dealing with young men like Royce. His flight schools had trained over 7,000 pilots for the war. He had convinced the Army to use small Piper planes that could take off and land in farm fields near the front lines. The winner of three international stunt flying events, Bevo was the first person to fly an outside loop in a lightweight plane.

"Well, a loop is nothing. You increase the throttle, pull the stick back. Then you just fly up, flip the belly of the plane over, and dive back down to get the plane horizontal with the ground—just like flying straight ahead. You just fly in a circle. Centrifugal force keeps you in your seat. It's pretty to watch. My grade school was still operating and I would fly down in a plane over the school, buzz the school. I was flyin' a P-T 19, open cockpit. The kids would all run out and I would put on a little airshow for them. They clapped and hollered."

Just because flying came easily to Royce, it didn't give him a free pass to do whatever he wanted. *"Bevo Howard was having an air show. When he finished the show, all the planes were leaving. When they left, they'd buzz the field, runnin' low on top of the cars. Bevo was the leader, other planes were following him. Even though I wasn't supposed to, I just followed suit. I didn't have that experience—supposedly. That was out of the book. I was flyin' in a big ol' Stinson then. Damn, if I didn't get grounded by a world champion stunt flyer because I was being a show-off!"*

Royce's fearlessness in the air impressed a successful business owner who himself was learning to fly. Once again, just the right mentor came into Royce's life at the perfect time. *"After I graduated from Hawthorne, I worked for them gassing the planes. That's where I met Britt. Everybody was flyin' everywhere then. Britt rented a plane and asked if I wanted to go up with him. He bought the gas. He took me up, tried to scare me by doin' some simple aerobatics, some loops. That's the easiest thing to do, a loop. You don't even fall against the belt. He asked me if I wanted to take over the* controls. *I said, 'Well sure.' I did some flying that's kind of tricky. I did a slow roll and a loop. Did another deal where you start like you're going to go into a loop, then you do a snap roll when you get to the top of the loop. Here you reverse the rudders, snap the stick, and you'll turn right-side-up because normally you'd be upside down at the top of a loop. Britt had no idea how much flyin' I'd done. One of my instructors was a fighter pilot during the war who'd taken me up in a PT-19 and had showed me a few maneuvers. After we were back on the ground, Britt said, 'Come work for me, I got a construction company.' I told him that I didn't have any experience. I was just a farm boy. I didn't know anything about what he was doing and I didn't have any work clothes, just had old khakis. He said he had decided and that he'd pick me up about 4:30 the next morning."*

Britt was true to his word, and before the sun reached the windows of Royce's room in his mother's unlocked boarding house in Columbia, Royce's eyes opened to a man he had never seen before. *"At four o'clock the next morning this guy come up the front stairs and into my bedroom and just woke me up. He took me to Orangeburg, South Carolina. They were building Quonset Huts with brick fronts for the Chrysler-Plymouth dealership. I decided right then to go to work for Britt."*

With a new wardrobe and the confidence to match, Royce was in charge of his own construction project within a month after going to work for H.A. Britton. Before the war, Britt, originally from Hugo, Oklahoma, had worked on mammoth construction projects in South America, casting public stadiums out of concrete. Now Britt owned his own construction company.

"After a month, I had my first big job. I was in charge of a project, supervising brick masons. I didn't know anything about laying brick. We were working on a big show room with plate glass windows. There was a front door with brick on either side. I acted like I knew more than those two brick masons. It started to rain, and they said we can't lay the brick because they're wet. I'm kind of bossy. I said, 'Bullshit. Make that thing work.' We went to lunch, came back, and that brick that was runnin' about eight feet high was swayin'. The masons had to

tear 'em down and re-do it. I'll never forget that. That's where I learned about brick."

The challenge to learn how to build whatever the project required expanded the skills of the former flight engineer. *"I could learn about all kinds of construction from Sweets Catalogue"* a resource that has transitioned from paper to a comprehensive website still providing technical information about building products. *"If I see somebody do something, I could do it. Like when I was eight years old, I'd watch the men, figure out how to do things. Anytime I see anything, I can look at a project and see how to make it work."*

After the War, new construction projects boomed. Royce and Britt were always looking for opportunities. *"We stopped at a little store out in the country, Crossroads. A guy had a big barn behind him there. We asked him about some work, and he said no, he didn't really need anything at that time, didn't need any concrete work. So help me, this is true, one of his guys come runnin' in there and says, 'Boss, the barn's on fire!' All the damned hay and everything, burned the damned barn down. There was an eight-foot concrete wall that the wooden barn sat on. So we got a concrete job. That was kind of neat. Right place, right time."*

Royce quickly felt a bond with Britt. He was learning a great deal about the construction business and gaining experience that could create a career well suited for him. But this wasn't enough to calm the temper of a twenty-four-year-old Royce. *"We were just beginning to do tilted up concrete, a new thing. Britt had asked me to go check out a new project that was going on in town, a telephone building five-stories high. I had gone to the sight to learn how they were doin' it and to see how we could improve it. I thought I would work on the next big job we had lined up. Well, Britt gave our next new job to his girlfriend's brother and that pissed me off because Britt and I were just father-son almost. We were real buddies. We traveled together, ate together. I drove his 1942 Plymouth so he could sleep while we were drivin'. And he gave the damn job to his girlfriend's brother. That pissed me off, of course. I said 'piss on that,' so I quit. I'd probably been with Britt for a year. He was a brain."*

Royce's hasty decision to leave his job with Britt cut off a good income in a business that was on the right side of the law. "That's one of the goofs on my part. After I left Britt, I started bootlegging again. I moved in with my mom, built a still, run it. I had my customers. I'd been there all my life. It was easy to get back in. But I got tired of that shit real quick. Aunt Belle knew what I was doing and she didn't like it. I came by her house and told her I was quittin'. She was so happy about that. I told her I was gonna quit moonshining and go back in the service. Yes, she was tickled about that."

CHAPTER 13
Gas Stations in the Sky

After Royce's re-enlistment, he would never again live in the South. Instead, he would explore every opportunity he could in the capital city of the state located in the geographic middle of the Union: Topeka, Kansas. *"When I walked into the station in Columbia to re-enlist, they gave me my same rank. I wanted to go back to England. They sent me to Forbes Field in Topeka. The guy at the enlistment office told me I'd be able to go to England again in a few weeks. So, I took a train to Topeka. It was years before we went to England."*

In Topeka, Royce immediately began work on an airplane new to him, the B-29. Used exclusively in the Pacific Theater during the War, this plane could reach heights of nearly 32,000 feet. Unlike the Liberator, the flight engineer on the B-29 had his own instrument panel. It would be a while before Royce got to feel the flight engineer's controls.

"*When I got to Forbes, I started working on the line as a mechanic on the B-29. The first time I walked out on the line, I saw a big pile of shit laying there. It was the pieces for a Quonset Hut. I'd been building those with Britt. I knew all about them. So, here's Royce again—I explained to them about how to put the Hut together. Long story. Anyway, I started working on the flight line. I could pull the cylinders off the plane. I could do that when a lot of people couldn't because my hands were so small—I could reach back in those cylinders. They got safety bolts there. Would safety the nut to the bolt, twist the wire, turn it a certain way so it can't come loose.*"

The differences between the B-24 and B-29 are made clear by Flight Engineer Fulmer, "*Oh goodness, it was like a Chevrolet and a Cadillac! The B-29 was a classic. It looked like the B-17. It was a beautiful airplane, but the engines weren't worth a shit at first. Had Pratt and Whitney on the B-24 and those SOBs run forever. You could work on them, but the early B-29 had a different engine. They were for long missions over water when we were bombing Japan, stationed on some island in the Pacific, a long-range thing. Their engines, however, weren't holding up very well."*

As Royce worked to keep the B-29s in the air, new applications for this plane, nick-named the "Superfortress," were being developed. The Cold War was on the horizon and the United States military knew little about the aviation capabilities of the Soviet Union. American planes were sent to probe the borders of the Iron Curtain to see if there would be a response. As tensions grew, the U.S. began running reconnaissance flights beyond the borders. The challenge became how to keep the planes fueled on these long and presumably secret flights.

"Why re-fuel a plane in the air? Where you gonna land them? Our jets were flying over the Soviet Union. They needed to extend their stay while they were photographing Russia. Didn't have fields to land those jets. Yes, refueling was a real interesting deal. Quite an accomplishment." Once again, Royce found himself on an unusual, even unprecedented assignment.

"*I was working on the ground crew, but I went on a couple assignments with air refueling. I got to go up in the air again because I qualified to go to the B-29 flight engineering school at Chanute Field in Rantaul, Illinois. Passed that exam with flying colors. Made a 92. When the B-24 first came off the assembly line, it had a panel for the flight engineer. But they took that off when we went to war. The B-29 has a station with a full set of controls. I graduated from Rantaul and went back to Forbes. This was the time when we were experimenting with air refueling. Those deals were some of the very first with the hoses. There were two crews doing that. When we first started, we'd hook the two planes together with a hose. You'd shit your britches seein' how we did this at first. We were flying the B-29 and refueling the B-50s. The B-50 was the receiver so it would fly down low. The two planes would be in tight formation.*"

"Tight formation" is one way to describe how the airplanes transferred the highly flammable fuel; the hose that hooked the planes together was less than 300 feet long. "*The B-50 would let out a pan on the end of a cable out the back of the airplane. We would be on one side of him and we'd drop a lead weight*" *straight down to catch that pan and take it. We'd pull that pan in and hook the pan into the end of the hose and let it back out again. Then we'd hook up the hose and reverse the process—slid across and start pumping the gas into the receiver plane, the B-50. We were always flying above the B-50. When we were done transferring the gas, we'd pull the hose back in, unsnap the hose, and put the pan back on. We were just reversing the procedure. It was pretty hard to keep our plane, the B-29, in there. The pilot's legs would shake like crazy when he was pushin' on the rudder. The tail on the B-50 made that maneuver even worse; we had to make sure we were on top of that tail. Altitude wasn't a big deal, maybe five, ten thousand feet. That's how I got into the tanker business."*

Air refueling had not been developed sufficiently to use during World War II. But because applications for refueling had become apparent during the War, testing became a priority. By 1947, the Air Force had become a separate department from the Army. Coming up with something to replace the dangerous looped-hose method Royce's crew used became a priority for the new department. Royce's ninety-year-old eyes sparkle when describing his involvement in testing these improvements.

"They sent our crews from Forbes to Renton, Washington. They had modified some old B-29s there, put a boom on the back, had reversible props. A boom is a telescoping tube with wings on it. The boom operator had control of the wings. He had a little station in the plane where he'd sit or lay down and maneuver his handholds to operate the boom. He would position the boom over the receptacle. There was a short airfield there in Renton for our take off. There was two planes and we were in the first one. We checked the flaps, reversed the props, taxied back around, and took off. That was the first airplane the Air Force had with a boom on the back. It was the beginning of B-29 air refueling with a boom. Yes, I was the first flight engineer on the first test flight this airplane had. The night before our flight, Boeing had a big party for the mechanics, a big shindig there in Renton. We got to go. After our test run, we got in our plane, took off and headed for home." The Boeing Company had developed the first flying boom. This improvement made the transfer of fuel relatively safer and resulted in faster fuel transfer.

The move from line mechanic back to flight engineer on the newly modified refueling planes sparked Royce's social life. *"We could always cancel a date with 'I gotta fly tonight.' Flying always came first. I used that excuse the night I met my first wife. I'd become friends with a guy, John Williams. He'd been a gunner on a plane in the South Pacific, got shot up pretty bad. He always called me 'Slick.' He called me up one night and says, 'Slick, what are you doing tonight?' I was going with a schoolteacher who was going to pick me up that evening, so I told him I was busy. He wanted me to go with him to the NCO Club. Two sisters were going to be singing there. I'd seen them there a couple nights before. John told me he had a date for me—one of the singers—Mary. I said I'd take it. Got on the phone to the teacher and told her I wouldn't be able to pick her up because I'd be flying. Always had the flying deal. Mary and I started going out then. I got rid of the schoolteacher. One night on the way home, we'd been to a movie. Mary was drivin' us in her car. I'm not proud, I'll ride. The schoolteacher was driving her car with her new boyfriend and they saw us. That gal tried to run us off the road! No, I wasn't a catch. I was a dumb*

SOB. John and Mary's sister Ruthie got married. Ruthie was younger than Mary, so once she and John got married, they were on us all the time that we should marry. Mary and I got married as well, in the Catholic Church. I didn't want to get married. We didn't marry for love."

Royce's friend John Williams was now his brother-in-law. These new husbands were married to sisters who had gained a lot of attention for their vocal talents. Arthur Capper, the owner of nearly every media outlet in the area at the time, had relocated Mary and her sister Ruth Miccolis from St. Louis. Originally from a suburb of Chicago, the sisters moved to Missouri to work when they were only fourteen and sixteen.

"Mary and her sister were very popular on radio and early TV. They were really popular with the cowboys, Gene Autry, Roy Rogers. They had gotten a letter from the Grand Ole Opry to go with them. I believe it was Roy Rogers who'd come to town. It come time for Mary to perform and she was so nervous to walk on stage. That happened to her a lot. I shoved her out on stage, and so help me, once she broke on the other side, you'd never known she was

so scared. I believe that was the last big show she entertained."

Mary's nerves about performing extended to her husband's job as an Airman. According to Royce, she begged him to leave the service, but instead he and Mary were separated for many months. *"My service got extended almost a year with the Korean War. I finally got to go back to England—Manston—down by Canterbury. I lived on the base there. It was alright. We didn't fly every day. The weather had a lot to do with it. We had a good boom operator on our crew, Clairmont. He really knew his stuff. That was somethin' how the planes would meet in the air. We refueled mostly over France. We would fly a racetrack pattern at our arranged meeting point, waiting for the receiving plane, a RB-47. We'd be at 12,000 feet, a little higher even. When we'd get ready to hook up the hoses, the planes had to slow down. During the fuel transfer we would slope down, pick up speed. The receiver plane was getting heavier and we were getting lighter."*

The RB-47 Stratojet was used early in the Cold War to gather information about Soviet air defense radar systems. Flying in silence mostly at night, the jets with a crew of only three ran secret reconnaissance flights.

"The Cold War was on then and we were photographing Russia. The RB-47 was a photographic plane, a big one. It had a lot of equipment on it. The crew had people on it, two or three, running all that electronic equipment. To refuel these jets we'd connect out of the top of their cockpit. There was a windshield there and the nozzle would go right over the top of their heads. I never missed a flight while we were over there. We transferred more gas than any crew over there at the time."

The day-to-day work of refueling the jets spying on the Soviets did not have the same probability of danger that the Carpetbagger Missions did. *"No question about it, the Carpetbagger job was more dangerous than refueling. That air refueling deal went slick. When you got it going it was a no-brainer."*

A couple unusual things happened during Royce's second assignment in England. He had watched fuel gush on the ground when the team fueling the plane let the plane's center of gravity tip. As gas ran off the runway onto a nearby road, an Englishman on a motorcycle came on the scene—riding his bike—smoke flying on the fuel-soaked road. *"I watched what was happening, just shittin' in my britches. I was afraid that SOB was gonna catch the fuel on fire."* Fortunately, Royce's prediction didn't come true.

Natural elements could also cause danger for the airborne crew. *"We took off with a load of fuel in a damned snowstorm. I looked out my window and saw the biggest snowflakes I've ever seen. Suddenly there was a big bang and the cockpit filled up with smoke. My pilot, Cobb, says, 'What happened, Royce?' I looked all around, checkin' everything, then another 'bang!' I left my seat and came up between the pilot and co-pilot to look at their instruments and out the side and the front. The damn binding wire on the outside of the plane had melted off. The wire was there to deal with static electricity. There was no question about it, we had been struck by lightning. It was simple then, see. Now we got a problem to solve. We can't land with the amount of fuel we had—too heavy. Can't land without getting rid of the fuel. We flew for ten hours to lighten the airplane, burnt it up before it got dark. We landed in Liverpool, England. After we landed, we inspected the plane. There were two places off the right-hand side of the nose where it looked like the aluminum had been burned."*

Yet, the closest Royce ever came to death with any man he ever flew with involved an event that none of his fellow airmen ever knew happened. *"I haven't talked too much about this, but I don't see why I can't now. I was in England the second time. It was dark one morning before takeoff. We were taxiing out and I was going through my checklist. I had flipped my switches to check the alternators; there were two on each engine. None of the alternators had come on. We had an extra power source in the back of the plane, called 'em 'putt-putts.' When the alternators didn't come on, I said, 'You'd better call the tower. We're not going to make it.' We turned around and as we started back to the hard stand where we'd come out, I hit one switch, and the damned thing came on. I says, 'Okay, call the tower. I think we can make it.' I'm just flipping my switches. There's switches everywhere. We got four engines and two alternators for each engine. The pilot called the tower and says, 'The engineer says we can make it.'*

We taxied back out again. Went through the check list again. I flipped the switches again, on and off. I left them all off. The switches were a magnetic thing, see. That's why you flipped 'em. It would catch once in a while, see. Like a toggle on a grill. Went through the check list, 'ready, ready, ready.' So, we took off. That putt-putt was runnin' in the back, which is alright as that keeps the electrical runnin'. So, we took off down the damned runway, and just before the pilot called for flaps up, the goddamned lights dimmed. Oh, shit, I thought. I knew immediately what it was. I didn't know if those switches would come on or not. But I hit the switches, caught 'em before the putt-putt stalled out. Just caught that SOB. It was dark in the plane, see. My panel had little green switches, so I knew right where they were. I just hit the first one and it caught. If it hadn't of caught, we would have crashed. No question about it because we couldn't have gotten the gear up. Couldn't operate without that power. Nobody knew about it except me. Another second maybe we'd have stalled because we couldn't get the gear up. Shit, we'd have smeared that whole countryside with the whole crew. I'd have killed everybody there. That's the only time I ever goofed up real bad. I had told the pilot to call the tower and get in line for takeoff. When we were taxiing, I didn't worry about the putt-putt. The cockpit lights were on and everything, see. It was just instinct for me to hit that control panel. It was just not our time. But boy, that was the closest I've come to killing us. I've had other close calls, but shit, I was responsible for this. No question about it, the responsibility there was me."

Even without the benefit of the details of what was going on with his work, Mary's anxiety grew while Royce was in England. Her mental health spiraled downward. After nearly half-a-year living at the base in Canterbury, Royce was told to go see his commanding officer. What he was told surprised him. *"Mary had worked for old man Capper. He owned the local paper, radio, TV station. He had brought her to Topeka from St. Louis. Mary knew lots of people. Somehow, she had got to the governor and convinced him to have me transferred back to Topeka. Yes, I was pissed. I didn't want to leave my crew. But I came back and went to work at the base in the ground school at Forbes, teaching pilots how to do take offs and landings. Especially when you're* messin' with bombers, you may be traveling around the world. There are a lot of factors to think about. If there's asphalt, for example, it takes longer to run on a hot runway. I taught pilots things like that. It was about time for me to get discharged—but my First Lieutenant, he was my boss—he wanted me to stay in. He said he was sure he could get me to captain and then send me on to the B-36s. They needed engineers on those. I was kind of hopped up about it, but the B-36s had a bad engine and Mary didn't want me to go. I couldn't stay in the service with Mary. She wanted me to get out. She couldn't handle it. She was nervous about me flyin', even though she had married a pilot. I still had my private pilot's license. I was gonna do crop dusting after the service. I knew a guy who was doin' it. Yeah, that was the kind of stupid shit I was thinking. Well, I left the service, and it wasn't but two weeks later that a friend of Mary's asked me to go into real estate. 'Why don't you come work for me?' he said. That's how I got started here in Topeka in the real estate business."

CHAPTER 14
"There Comes My Heart Now"

After Royce left the service for the second time, he would spend the next sixty years developing commercial and residential real estate projects. The shoeless country boy from the Deep South would have tremendous success. He would also find himself dead broke several times. Not one to call himself an entrepreneur, *"I was more manure than anything else,"* Royce was always looking for the next big deal and wasn't afraid to gamble it all on the possibility of a big payoff.

"A friend got me a job with Bill Senogle's real estate company. I was workin' in the field then, drivin' around, looking for land. We would develop communities, put in the streets, sewers. I had a hell of

a time. That was a good deal. I was definitely making some money. I became a project manager pretty quick."

Having soaked up new knowledge about real estate development, Royce and another young developer, Keith Meyers, decided to go out on their own. *"I had taken a new job with a different company, The Sargent Company. Became a successful salesman there. Keith Meyers was working doing marketing. He knew his stuff. He had grown up poor. He was smart. He and I decided to share a little office where the Coke machine was. We really hit it off. One day he said, 'Royce, why don't we form our own company?' We decided to do it."*

Keith had seen a new concept for retail development on a trip to the East Coast. Fulmer and Meyers decided to take on additional investors and build the first indoor shopping mall in the capital city. *"We owned the land around the shopping center. Had office buildings, five or six of those. Built apartment buildings. We got into big-box stores, too. Had half-a-dozen K-Marts going. Got into Targets at the last. We made some really good bucks there. We bought a used Twin Beech Bonanza for $150,000.*

Had a pilot. Couldn't fly it ourselves because of the insurance. I'd go to a different place every day and supervise our projects. I had that goin' pretty good for a little bit. How was my home life then? It was not going anywhere, you might say."

Royce and Mary would have two sons. Their first son, born in 1954, was named Britt after the man whose brief appearance in Royce's life had made such an impact. Bobby was born six years later. Like their mother, both boys are musically talented. And like their father, both would become businessmen. Neither Royce's family nor his business with Keith would stay together.

"The shopping center became a mess. Keith was drinking at this point. I tried to help him a couple of times. When we split up, I paid him ten thousand dollars for some old office furniture. I had some land and started building lots of different projects. The bank financed me there. I had eighteen carpenters working for me building houses. My oldest son was in college. It was then I decided to leave Mary. I told her I would still support her. Gave her the house and everything in it. Only thing I took was an old green Naugahyde chair a decorator had given me 'cause I

sent her so much business. Wasn't even leather. I paid support to Mary for thirty-four years. I don't think she ever did really love me. She loved what I was doin', but I don't think she loved me. "

With a clean slate and empty bank accounts, Royce again began to re-build his business. He hired a petite, aggressive realtor named Bette Jackson. She would work for Royce for over thirty-five years, moving her over-sized desk every time R.A. Fulmer, Co. relocated its office to the garage of the current model home in the developments she sold for her boss. Decades of developments and deals meant lots of money made and lost.

"I was up and down. I'd dabble here, dabble there. I was making money like crazy there for a while. But then I put a restaurant in another shopping center I'd developed. Lost money on that deal. I had a lot of opportunities come my way. McDonalds begged us to help 'em. With Meyers and our partners, we put the first one in town on Topeka Boulevard. Remember that sign? Now it's in the Kansas History Museum. Yes, I did think about buying a franchise. But I had a good friend who owned a restaurant on 29th Street. He was known as

the 'Pickle King' here. He made his own dill pickles. He told me there was no way a guy could sell a damned hamburger like McDonalds was for twenty-five cents! No way they could make a go of it. I trusted him. The Pizza Hut guys, Frank and Dan Carney, brothers down from Wichita. Hell yes, I knew them. One of the brothers and I were gonna buy a bunch of land here, had a contract, but a guy undercut us. Had another opportunity with Kentucky Fried Chicken, but I passed on that."

There was one opportunity that as much as he tried to let it go, he just couldn't. "I had an office in the upstairs floor of a building I shared with a bunch of attorneys and an insurance agency. Karon worked for Keith Meyers in the building. She was, of course, cuter than shit. She took dictation, shorthand. She was a good secretary and so cute. I noticed that when we played gin sometimes after work, that she started pullin' for me. But shit, I was broke. I had just started making my support payments to Mary. I asked Karon out on a date. There was somethin' different there. I don't know why she fell in love with me. If there ever was a first sight type thing it was that. It didn't take me long til I knew I wanted to stay *with Karon. I don't know what the hell she loved me for. But Karon, she hung in there with me. First thing, I had to get past her folks. That took a year before I met them. They surprised me and accepted me pretty openly. I really loved her parents. Her dad and I would go out to eat every week and he would always pay. I respected him. I wished I had had a dad like him. I could tell Karon was happy. Yes, she does spoil me. I think she really loves me."*

Neither of them being superstitious, on Friday the 13th of February 1976, Royce and Karon were married by the Methodist pastor who had known Karon since she was a child growing up in the tiny town of Harveyville, Kansas. *"Getting married was just the thing to do. We never got upset with each other. She was smart, pretty. She loved me and I loved her. I did promise her children. I had some reserve there, my age. She thought that would be alright."*

Royce and Karon did have two children. A boy, Justin, was born in 1978. The engineering aptitude of his father was passed to Justin who applies his abilities in electronic technologies. In 1980, a daughter was born. Named after his mother, Royce was happy to be a dad for the fourth time. *"I always wanted a little girl.*" The second Lessie has the beauty of her grandmother, and to Royce's relief, intelligence that extended to her choice in a husband.

Though there were times when Royce's business would suffer cash flow problems, a relatively stable economy enabled him to find the next project. And sometimes money just seemed to drop out of nowhere exactly when it was needed. "*I was broke. I was looking at buying lots to build high-end duplexes, but I didn't have the cash to do it. I was seventy and I still wasn't drawing Social Security. A gal from Montgomery, Alabama called me and said, 'Royce Fulmer, I got a note here that we owe you some money.' I said, 'Oh? How much is it?' She said, 'Looks like $67,000 dollars.' So they sent me $67,000 I was owed in Social Security and I got started again. I got a new partner, bought more acreage next to the land I'd been lookin' at. Made a million dollars on that deal. I blew that too.*"

Though the standard of living he provided his family fluctuated, Royce had always been able to find his feet again. But when an eight trillion-budollar housing bubble burst in 2007, even the conservative Kansas housing market was rocked. The worst recession since Royce was just a boy created a problem for his business that he could not fix. Royce lost his business, his house, and had no money in the bank. He was eighty-six years old.

"I was sittin' in my office there, didn't know which way to jump. Didn't know what I was gonna' do. In comes Bob Zibell. I had sold him some duplexes for just under a million bucks a few years back. I knew he was an operator. I said, 'Shit, Bob, I'm broke.' He said get in the car with me and we'll go to Colorado. I left Bette with all my shit. Went to Steamboat Springs, Colorado with him. It gave me hope. I thought, well shit, I'll do this all again. I'd done it three times before."

Trying to get several projects off the ground in Colorado, Royce and Karon made the decision to live apart. Karon stayed in Kansas where her job as a high school special education para-educator gave her a regular paycheck and health insurance. She left the home Royce had built for her and moved into a basement room in a house that belonged to Bob and his wife. Royce lived in Colorado in another basement room in a second house owned by the couple.

"*That was bad, living apart from Karon. I wasn't eating much. I hated us not being together. I'd been working with Bob in Colorado for about a year, trying to get several deals goin'. We had gone to Denver to a bankruptcy sale. We bid on some property. It was a good location, but we didn't get it. Well, that kind of put the rag on the bush right there. I had just had too much. I finally faced up to the fact that I'd screwed up. I had a tightness in my chest when we were in Denver. The morning after we'd drove back to Steamboat Springs, I decided to walk from the house to the Come & Go to get me a chilidog. Bob was gonna go to the airport to fly his wife to The Badlands because her mom was in the hospital. I walked down to the store, looked at the food, but didn't get it. My chest was still tight. I saw Bob and his wife at the store. They drove me back to the house. I told them I was gonna go inside and lay down for a bit and rest. I went into my room. I was alone in the house. I realized then I was in trouble. I actually saw a big damn light—a circle—shining like a prism. It was a few feet off the ground, few feet in diameter. I wanted to tell Karon good-bye. I was gonna write her a note and tell her that I loved her and that I was sorry I screwed up. I was up and around looking for something to write on."* With a laugh Royce continues, *"I couldn't find a pencil or a goddamn piece of paper! So instead, I called Bob and he come right on when I hit his number. I was in trouble. I knew I was in trouble. I said, 'Bob, I've got a problem.' I'd never said that to anybody before. He was taxiing in his plane out to takeoff. Normally you don't answer the phone when you are taxiing out for takeoff. For some reason he answered his phone. Bob called the ambulance and he rushed back to the house to meet them. I could hear them coming down the stairs, but by that time all I saw was a big damn light. I could hear them talking, but that was about it. The ambulance guy started doing something to me right away."*

Never losing consciousness, Royce heard the emergency room doctor talking to Bob. *"The doctor told Bob, 'We can't do anything for this guy here.' I thought, 'Well shit, school's out!' I had no vision—could hear—but I couldn't see. Bob called for the helicopter and they took me up to Loveland; happened to be a brand-new, first-rate heart center. They took me there on a helicopter. I was laying down in there. By now I could see out of the corner of my eyes. I could see we were going through the mountains. We were flying fairly low. It wasn't a very long flight, maybe thirty minutes. Well yes, I did enjoy the flight. The next day I was feeling pretty decent. I'd had a stent put in before and this time a blood clot formed on the end of the stent. I talked to the doctor there and told him I had to go back to work. The doctor said the first thing I had to do was get out of the hospital. Karon drove up and got me, said she was takin' me home to Kansas. Weak, yeah, I guess I was bad. But you know, I've had the worst luck and the best luck. Have you ever seen that much of a spectrum? Yes, I've had a real complex life."*

EPILOGUE
"Thank You for Your Service"

Seven years before the heart attack that would force him to reluctantly retire, Royce built a house for my family that had now grown to four sons. I hadn't planned on building a new home. All I had done was stop by my neighbor's office in the garage of his latest model home. I asked Royce if he had any ideas about how I could make my laundry room more functional. *"You won't be happy until you have a new house!"* I think I remember a wink following this proclamation. It may be that my memory has just inserted one. With blueprints tucked under my arms of *"the best house I've ever built for a big family,"* I went home to tell my patient husband that maybe we should think about selling our house.

On the long walks I watched Royce start on with his dog, he had explored a piece of land just up the hill from our neighboring homes. He must have been reminded of his childhood. The land has a creek running through it. Parts of it are almost like a forest, or at least as close as Kansas can come to one. Cottonwood trees stand tall on this land, shimmering with sound when the familiar winds blow through. Not an obvious building site for a house, Royce envisioned bringing in truckloads of excavated dirt from basements he dug to create a perfect elevation. In his mind he engineered a complex yet reliable system to install a pump, underground pipe, and connecting lateral field to avoid septic tank failure for the new home he wanted to build. *"I want to do this for your family before I die."*

Royce was right. The home he built for us works beautifully for our family. And the "deal" we got on it did not go unnoticed by my husband and myself. Yet I missed sharing a property line with Royce and Karon. We saw them often but didn't share the same daily rhythms when we were next door to each other.

With growing sons, life grew even busier for us. I knew Royce and Karon were facing difficulties. My mother and I often discussed how much we hated the couple living apart. Seeing him after his heart attack sobered me to the fact that the vibrant man who my children held out as an example of how they wanted to age, was in fact, slowing down.

So, it was with some reservation that I called Karon and asked her about having Royce help me with some projects for my house. She made it clear she thought it would be great for him to have a project. Almost immediately Royce was teaching my oldest son how to operate power tools needed to build sturdy shelves for the garage. *"You need to feel the tools in your hands. Even if you don't make things yourself, you'll better appreciate the work others do."*

My casual mention that dirt was eroding into the creek resulted in the creation of two wooden barricades. They were filled with new dirt that is now held snugly in place. Building these walls in the middle of a Kansas summer was sweaty work. I brought Royce cold water and a chair to sit on and rest. He insisted he was *"doin' just great."* Relaxing in the chair, his attention turned to the overgrown path leading into the woods. As his student on this project, he showed me the correct way to cut protruding branches. I learned to properly stack them in a pile we would burn in the fall after the wood had dried.

I looked forward to Royce coming to the house to work on the projects. We would sit and talk before he and my son would begin their work, "*Just a half-a-cup of coffee, there now.*" He surprised me when he wondered out loud if he was nearing the end of his life because so many old memories, long tucked away, flooded his mind before sleep. I began to realize the man who had become such a dear friend, more a brother really, had more life experiences than I had ever begun to imagine.

That summer, a late-night drive from the airport on our way home from vacation was interrupted with a text from Karon. Royce was in the hospital and he wasn't doing well. For the next two and a half weeks, Royce would lay in his hospital bed refusing to eat, telling everyone around him "*just let me sleep.*" We were relieved when tests came back negative but grew more perplexed by his loss of interest in life. He came home and stayed in his bed in a cozy room that smelled of familiar coffee-scented candles. His voice grew weak and he would barely lift his head from the pillow. His daughter was close to delivering her first child. Yet Royce, weak from not eating, had given up on having a future. The airman who always eased quickly to sleep, now found his nights interrupted with dreams that became hallucinations. Sleepless herself for several nights in a row, I insisted to Karon that I spend the night at her house so she could get some rest. Royce had become more active and we were concerned he might get out of his bed. With his room on the second floor, we worried he might fall down the stairs. I promised Karon I would watch her husband. Propped in his doorway with the familiar comfort of quilts sewn by grandmothers, I watched my dear friend through the night. His hands were busy working on projects only he could see. He talked about three-legged cats and blood on the wall. But mostly, he wanted Karon. Hours before dawn, I woke her. Still exhausted, she came to his bed and Royce calmed for a time.

As Royce finally drifted to sleep, Karon and I agreed that hospice needed to be called. Almost immediately, a nurse was talking with Royce in a loving but no-nonsense manner. She confirmed to me privately that it was right to call and that she would not leave until we had arranged care for him.

We were concerned about how we would get him safely down the stairs to the van that would take Royce to the building where we assumed he would die. I waited downstairs while the men with the van talked to Royce in his second-floor room. Time made no sense to my sleepless mind. Perhaps it was minutes before I saw Royce, dressed in a T-shirt, jeans, and sandals, walk down the stairs without the help of anyone else. The men who had been there to carry him now waited at the bottom of the stairs. Royce safely reached them and was greeted by the older of the two men with a salute. "Thank you for your service," the man said. The hospice nurse, the aide who helped Royce, Karon, and I, all fought a losing battle with tears.

But Royce doesn't live life the way most people do. Five days after being admitted to hospice, he was lovingly kicked out and sent home. Royce met his new grandson, a milestone that just weeks before seemed unlikely. The school year began and Karon returned to work, comforted in the knowledge that Royce was looked after by his aide Deb and visited often by friends and family.

By early spring Royce was out of his bed, voice strong, and once again back to his life-long habit of exercising. Like the dormant flowers emerging from the dead of winter, I could see Royce growing stronger. I had teased Royce for years that his life deserved a book. With everything he had done for me and my family, I felt compelled to be the person to help make that a reality. Armed with an inexpensive voice recorder, a new notebook, and a sense that we had been given the gift of time, Royce and I sat down on the blue flowered couch his wife is so ready to replace, and started our project. He teases me about my enthusiasm for his life story. *"You're just a goddamned optimist,"* he tells me. I'm sure there was a wink that time. He's right. I am an optimist. And if anyone ever taught me the value of this view of life, it's Royce Alton Fulmer.

POSTSCRIPT

"Hey, Royce—we've got to get going soon," I said to my writing partner who laid in his bed snuggled between soft, flannel sheets. "The men at the 190th are expecting us at 2:00." It was 1:25. I knew the drive would take at least 15 minutes.

"Well just hold on," Royce said. "I need to shower and shave before we go."

Immediately I realized my not-so-subtle encouragement should have been made much sooner. Royce had begun to slow down. He slept for long stretches of time during the day. He wasn't eating much. Even his favorite, Karon's ham-n-beans, couldn't rouse his appetite. It was more difficult for him to catch his breath. Royce had reluctantly agreed to use oxygen. My feeble attempt to compare the pronged tube placed in his nose to the days when he needed supplemental air on high altitude flights was admittedly ridiculous.

It had been well over a year since the hospice nurse came to Royce's home the first time. She now visited him twice a week. Despite the emotional hazards of falling in love with her patients, she clearly adored Royce. Watching the two of them spend time together felt more like visits enjoyed with family. I smile when I remember Royce greeting his nurse with a hug and then leading her in a few dance steps. Amidst the laughter, there were also matter-of-fact discussions about the progression of his aging body. He processed the information like a flight engineer: taking in data, analyzing it, accepting the conclusion. There was never any fear.

Royce's nurse was consulted regarding an invitation Royce received to tour the 190th Air Refueling Wing of the Kansas Air National Guard. She enthusiastically encouraged him to go if he felt he could. The story of Royce's life as told through this book had received the attention of a local newspaper reporter. Royce was to be interviewed and photographed as the featured serviceman for the

Veteran's Day edition of the paper. Though not sure he was deserving of all the attention, Royce enjoyed talking with the reporter and posing for the photographer in a blue wingback chair. Days later, his picture splashed on the front of the *Topeka Capital Journal*, Royce quipped, "Well, I never had that happen before."

The story of Royce's secret mission and subsequent test flights in the early days of air refueling caught the attention of the men and women of the 190th Air Refueling Wing, located on the same spot, or at least a portion of it, where Royce served nearly 70 years ago. Surprised to learn that one of the pioneers of air refueling lived in the same city, an invitation was extended to Royce and myself to be their guests for a tour.

"Royce, you've got to hurry or we'll be late," I said, trying to conceal my worry.

"Don't be so anxious," a clean-shaven Royce said to me. Karon had laid out his outfit: jeans, a blue chambray shirt, and a black, lambskin leather jacket. I encouraged him to wear his "World War II Veteran" baseball cap my stepfather had purchased at the VA. Royce's nurse suggested he take a dose of morphine before we left the house. Royce pointed out to me that portable oxygen and airplane fuel "don't mix well." The morphine would help his mind relax and makes breathing feel easier.

"It's easy for you to tell me not be anxious," I say as I start the car, glancing at the dash clock that proves I am right to worry we'll be late. "I'm not the one on morphine!"

We laugh and I focus my mind to make sure I remember the best route to the Airbase. Though I have no real proof, or even far-out theory, I have always believed that when the sun is shining in Kansas, there is no sky more blue or more beautiful. The day we drive to the Airbase is one of those days.

As we pull into Forbes Field, we are greeted at the front entrance by retired planes perched on stands to look as though they are in flight. Forbes is no longer used by the Air Force. It houses the Kansas Air National Guard, commercial buildings, and a couple of military museums. Teenagers just learning to drive are brought here by nervous parents as the once-busy streets are now mostly quiet. Many buildings sit empty, decaying.

"This is World War II veteran and guest of honor Royce Fulmer; we're expected," I say to the young man at the gated entrance to the 190th. I immediately realize how corny I sound. Thankfully, Royce has brought his wallet. After an inspection of our driver's licenses, we are allowed in.

The Master Sergeant is waiting for us, his car parked just inside the gate. He motions to us to follow. I accelerate to keep up with him as we drive past several buildings on our way to the airplane hangar. The officers at the 190th have been told Royce is weak. I have been instructed to drive into the hanger. Approaching the entrance, we see over a dozen uniformed Airmen. One motions for us to enter the long tunnel into the hanger. I drive into a wide hallway, the floor perfectly clean and the lights bright.

Driving slowly to the doors at the end of the tunnel I blurt out, "Oh man, I can't cry in front of these guys!"

"Hell, I think *I'm* gonna cry," responds Royce, which only makes my tears more likely.

I look at the clock in my car. We are eight minutes late. My stepfather, a retired Army Colonel who today is dressed more like a college professor, has arrived early to tell the Airmen who this fellow Royce is.

Warmed by a brief biography of their guest, the Airmen walk alongside my car until we reach the end of the tunnel. I turn off the car. Immediately Royce, who just minutes ago had to be roused from his bed, jumps from the passenger seat when the car door is opened for him. Snapping to attention, he salutes the Escort Officer. Amid the laughter and welcomes, I'm glad I stuffed a Kleenex in my pocket.

We enter the hanger. It is the largest room I have ever been in. Royce is at home. Standing just a few feet from a KC-135 air refueling plane, Royce begins to tell his audience about his early days in air refueling. He is modest about his accomplishments, so his stories are supplemented by me and my stepfather. There is a collective gasp when my stepdad tells the active duty airmen that Royce's crew brought gas to Patton's tanks. I ask Royce later if that embarrassed him. "I just wish ya woulda' told it twice," he said.

Royce is invited to board the plane. Unlike his Liberator whose belly hovered close to the ground, there is a long flight of stairs that Royce must climb to reach the plane's entrance. I am concerned how Royce will climb the platform; he climbs it too quickly for me to keep up.

"I love the smell of airplanes," Royce says as he breathes deeply after climbing the stairs. An Airman replies to Royce, "That's hydraulic fuel, the same red goop that was used in your day."

The exterior of the plane is painted gray. Built in 1960, the aircraft is in the process of having two engines replaced. Royce steps into the interior of the plane. It is empty though seats can be installed if needed. We stand on a metal floor also painted gray. The rubber tanks that hold the fuel for transfer are below our feet. For the first time since he leapt from my car, Royce is silent. Smiling, he walks to the other side of the plane to an open door exposing the wing on the co-pilot's side of the plane. He asks a young Airman, "How long is that wing?" Royce expects a quick answer and is given one.

The bright interior lights of the plane do not extend to the tail of the craft, the area where the boom operator does his work. Royce is invited to climb down into the boom pod. I nervously glance down at the couch, the narrow area where the boom operator lays on his belly to fly the boom. My step-father whispers to me that he will spot Royce as I watch my 91-year-old friend climb down into the pod. I catch a glimpse of him on his belly, head raised high, as he talks with the boom operator who is also hunkered in the pod. Long minutes later, Royce climbs out with minimal assistance.

Royce is the most animated I have seen him in months. Safely out of the pod, he notices a box-shaped piece of equipment near the tail. It is about four-by-four feet in dimension. I share what I've been told. "That's the auxiliary power unit, Royce. A modern putt-putt." I'm convinced he thinks about the B-29 flight where his plane nearly lost power.

"I sure could a used one of those things!" Royce says with a laugh.

The Airmen are surprised to learn that Royce's auxiliary power source ran on gasoline. They appreciate the danger of a gas-powered device in a moving plane.

"You guys are showing me Heaven before I get there," Royce says as he walks to the cockpit.

Royce is not disappointed by what he is shown at the nose of the plane. A pilot who must be close to Royce's grandson's age, and even shares a resemblance to a young Royce, shows Royce a picture on his phone of the cockpit's high-tech instrumentation panel at night. Royce shakes his head in admiration of the rack of computers he's told replaces the plane's navigator. Naïvely I ask, "Where does the flight engineer sit?" Glances are exchanged and someone says, "Well, about ten years ago we stopped using in-flight engineers. If we have a problem, we take a picture and send it to an engineer on the ground." Royce shakes his head even longer as he hears that the plane is now operated by just three Airmen: a pilot, co-pilot, and boom operator.

Saying he could just stay and "sleep in the cockpit tonight," Royce reluctantly departs the plane, his gait strong, his face flushed pink. Safely on the concrete floor of the hanger, he is given two patches by the Master Sergeant. There is no need to coax a smile from him as pictures are taken. He's had a grin on his face since we entered the hanger.

Sitting in a chair close to the plane, Royce signs copies of his book for every man present. It is obvious that Royce does not want to leave, but when told we "need to clear the area," the former Airman nods and quickly moves toward the exit door. Several men help Royce into the car more out of respect than necessity.

As we leave the base, I drive slowly, savoring the last few moments we have at this place. "You know," Royce says, looking out the car window, "I really think they are going to remember me."

A little over a month after our visit to the 190th, Royce's final days were spent at the VA close to his home. Karon took time off from work and stayed with him constantly, leaving only for short nights of sleep or necessary errands. Visits from family and friends were full of many laughs and a few tears. Royce only laughed.

"You know," Royce told me shortly before his health required him to leave his home, "this may sound crazy, but I'm *excited* about my future."

"I'm fine, I'm fine," was the last thing he said to me, a little more than a day before he died. And I knew he was. After all, Royce had been telling me for weeks now, "I'm going to join God's Air Force!"

The official picture of the Borden Crew taken at their top-secret base near Harrington, England in the fall of 1944. Back row from right to left: Pilot William L. Borden, Navigator Jack P. Barton, Co-Pilot Veron L. Doran, Bombardier James D. Bruning. Front row right to left: Radio Operator Max E. Dinsmore, Flight Engineer Royce A. Fulmer, Dispatcher Harry P. Kieschnick, Tail gunner Stacy V. Phillips.

The original Borden Crew taken shortly after they were assembled at Peterson Field in Colorado. They would travel across the Atlantic together, but after given their top-secret mission, two of the gunners would be reassigned. Back row from left to right: Flight engineer Royce A. Fulmer, Radio Operator Max E. Dinsmore, Dispatcher Harry P. Kieschnick, Ball Gunner who was later reassigned, Gunner who was reassigned, Tail Gunner Stacy V. Phillips. Front Row left to right: Navigator Jack P. Barton, Pilot William L. Borden, Bombardier James D. Bruning and Co-Pilot Vernon L. Doran.

B-24 flight engineer Royce Fulmer while participating in the top-secret mission "Operation Carpetbagger."

Tail gunner Stacy Phillips in his fleece-lined bomber jacket. Royce and Stacy are the only surviving Borden Crew members at the time of this writing.

Operation Carpetbagger had an official photographer who must have been the person who captured this photo on secret base 179 near Harrington, England. Royce is seen in the front, kneeling, Thanks to gunner Stacy Phillips, on the far left, for sharing this rare photo. Radio operator Dinsmore is in the middle. The man on the far right helped load the supplies onto the Liberators. The photo was taken during the record-breaking cold winter of '44-'45.

Pilot William L. Borden. This picture is taken from the cover of his book, *There will be No Time, The Revolution in Strategy.* Borden wrote the book after the War, before he attended Yale Law School

Model maker Bill Eggerling, LTC (ret), began with a commercial model purchased from Revell, a 1-48 scale. This photo is the cutaway starboard half of the fuselage showing how the B-24 Liberator was reconfigured for use in Operation Carpetbagger. The core of the wing, the core of the horizontal stabilizer, the majority of the bulkheads, the right open position, and the aircraft ribs throughout the plane were built from scratch.

This photo shows the cockpit, the radio operator's position, and the top turret which was the flight engineer's gun position if, as Royce put it, "there was a possibility of a problem." The area below the radio operator's position was used for storage of the pannier containers.

This photo emphasizes the open bomb bay where the C-containers would have been mounted on the four vertical racks in the bomb bay. To the right of the bomb bay is the Joe Hole. A spy trained to aid the Resistance is sitting there, preparing to jump into Nazi-occupied territory. As a result of Operation Carpetbagger, over 1,000 men and several dozen women parachuted from Carpetbagger Liberators.

This photo features a built-from-scratch auxiliary power unit (APU) or, as Royce calls, it the "putt-putt." The APU was in every B-24.

Production and packing of supplies dropped to Resistance fighters was a complex operation. At a secret location, in an isolated wooded area 50 miles from Operation Carpetbagger's base, American soldiers worked around the clock packing the dangerous materials that would be tossed out of the moving B-24 Liberator. 20,495 C-containers and 11,174 panniers were dropped with supplies critical in the fight against Hitler and his forces. The containers were outfitted with shock-absorbing material on one end in an effort to improve the safety of dropping gasoline, blood plasma and grenades, for example, from a moving Liberator airplane. This picture represents the ground crew responsible for loading the supplies into the plane. Unlike other ground crews working the planes assigned to bomber missions, these men had the benefit of daylight for their work.

Royce in uniform while stationed at Forbes Field in Topeka, Kansas. This was during an extension of his enlistment due to the Korean War. At this time, he was the flight engineer on the B-29 on some of the earliest re-fueling fights for the Air Force. When Royce left the Air Force in August of 1952 he was 29 years old.

Royce in his late teens in South Carolina.

Royce's mother, Lessie Mae.

Royce in the early years of his career as a real estate developer in Topeka, Kansas.

Additional photos and information about Royce can be found on Facebook: A Drop in the Night.

Notes on Sources

Chapter 1: Necessity Invents a Top-Secret Mission

Thea wants to thank Chaplain (Colonel) George Pejakovich, USA Retired, graduate of the U.S. Military Academy at West Point, New York 1967, for his tremendous help and encouragement with this project. He patiently helped me understand the military and historical information needed to tell Royce's story.

In gathering historical information, I found the BBC history website helpful: *BBC News*. BBC, 21 Aug. 2014. Web. 25 Aug. 2014.

Much has been written about the Marquis. For example, see: "Spartacus Educational." *Spartacus Educational*. N.p., n.d. Web. 25 Aug. 2014.

If you are new to the study of World War II, and don't mind carrying around a book with a demeaning title, you will find a compelling overview from Mitchell G. Bard, Ph.D. *The Complete Idiot's Guide to World War II, Third Edition* (Penguin Group, 2010).

Chapter 2: "While I Breathe, I Hope"

The economic difficulties facing South Carolina even before the Great Depression are discussed at: *www.teachingushistory.org/lessons/The1920s-NotRoaringinSouthCarolina.html*.

The gritty realities of share cropping in the South are explored at: *www.pbs.org/tpt/slavery-by-another-name/themes/sharecropping/.*

A video of the use of a scythe in the field can be found at: *www.youtube.com/watch?v=AqbcqthUZb8*

To see Poole's FBI Most Wanted Poster: *www.fbimostwanted.us/zc/index.php?main_page=p roduct_info&products_id=298.*

Chapter 3: "Runnin' Whiskey"

Despite early denials, NASCAR now officially embraces the link between bootleggers and early drivers: *http://www.nascar.com/en_us/news-media/articles/2012/11/01/moonshine-mystique.html.*

The school where Royce earned his engine license to work on planes was featured in a local newspaper during the War. The second article on this page mentions Bevo Howard, the owner of the flight school where Royce got his pilot's license: *www.dspace.ychistory.org/bitstream/handle/11030 /70142.*

Though they were divorced at the time of their deaths, Aunt Belle and Uncle Reeder share a burial plot: *www.image1.findagrave.com/photos/2008/239/293 43101_121986879136.jpg/00000024.pdf?sequence=1*

Chapter 4: The Making of a Soldier

If you love airplane history, there is a fascinating training video produced by the Federal Government during WWII about how to fly the B-24: *www.zenoswarbirdvideos.com/B-24.html*.

Once top secret, you can now read the operations manual for the B-24 at: *www.avialogs.com/list/item/3866-pilot-training-manual-b-24-the-liberator-part-1-2*.

For a great read about Liberator Pilot and Senator George McGovern that details his experiences running daytime bombing raids during the war, see: Stephen E. Ambrose, *The Wild Blue, The Men and Boys Who Flew the B-24s Over Germany 1944-45.* (Simon & Schuster, Reprinted 2002).

Chapter 5: "Crewin' Up!"

The history of the many military bases used to train WW II soldiers is often well documented. This is true in the case of Peterson Army Airbase, the base where Royce and his crew met: *www.petemuseum.org/peterson-air-force-base-history/*.

Attempts were made to contact surviving family of each member of the Borden crew. Despite the passage of nearly seventy years since their mission ended, three families helped contribute. We would like to sincerely thank Stacy V. Phillips, his wife Liz, and their son Kent. It was a powerful moment to hear flight engineer Fulmer and gunner Phillips reunite on the phone after sixty-nine years. Thanks go to Rich Barton, son of navigator Jack P. Barton and to Mary Bruning, daughter-in-law of bombardier James D. Bruning for their willingness to answer a call from a stranger in Kansas and their encouragement on this project.

Chapter 6: Off We Go

The history of early trans-Atlantic flight is discussed at: *www.aircrew-saltire.org/lib120.htm.*

Chapter 7: Mission Revealed

For those who are interested in exploring Operation Carpetbagger in great detail, see: Ben Parnell, *Carpetbaggers: America's Secret War in Europe* (Eakin Press, 1987).

Prior to his death in 2008, the final commanding officer of the Carpetbagger mission, Col. Robert W. Fish, compiled stories from other Carpetbaggers: *www.801492.org/Air%20Crew/They%20Flew%20By%20Night(sm).pdf.*

In 1993, Englishman Bernard Tebbutt did an amazing thing. He decided to create the Carpetbagger Aviation Museum on his land, the site of Station 179. This project now supports not only the museum, but hosts many events and produces a newsletter, all dedicated to preserving the important history of the Carpetbagger Mission: *www.harringtonmuseum.org.uk/WhatWeAre.htm.*

Chapter 8: The Work Begins

The Carpetbaggers helped solve a significant problem when they supplied General Patton with much needed gasoline: *www.qmfound.com/pol.htm.*

The dangers posed by German Night Fighters to the Allies is well documented: *www.historylearningsite.co.uk/german_night_fight ers.htm.*

Chapter 9: "Churchill's Secret Army"

Female spies in WW II are finally receiving recognition long deserved: *www.express.co.uk/news/uk/386800/Churchill-s-heroines-How-Britain-s-female-secret-agents-changed-the-course-of-WWII.*

For an excellent book on the accomplishments of women spies, see: Ann Kramer, *Women Wartime Spies* (MJF Books, 2011).

Chapter 10: Lost and Found

An interview of a surviving member of the Berkhoff crew is found at:
www.altoonaherald.desmoinesregister.com/article/20130113/IOWAHEROES/301130010/A-Salute-WWII-Veterans-Jack-Webb-focus

Chapter 11: Headin' Home

A review of Pilot Borden's book is found at: *www.ethanheilman.tumblr.com/post/29405762446/there-will-be-no-time-a-review.*

See the letter Borden wrote to J. Edgar Hoover regarding his concerns about Robert Oppenheimer: *www.mphpa.org/classic/JRO/01.htm.*

The impact Borden's views had on the life of Oppenheimer are recently discussed by Ray Monk, *Robert Oppenheimer, A Life Inside the Center* (Anchor Books, 2012).

Chapter 12: Figuring Things Out

World Champion stunt flyer and aeronautics pioneer Bevo Howard was killed in 1971 while flying in a charity fund-raising event: *www.spence-air-base.com/bevo.html.*

The plane Bevo flew at his fatal crash was restored and is on display at the Smithsonian National Air & Space Museum: *www.airandspace.si.edu/collections/artifact.cfm?object=nasm_A19731672000.*

Royce's construction business mentor, H.A. Britton, died in a car crash just a few years after Royce and he split up.

Chapter 13: Gas Stations in the Sky

Forbes Air Force Base has been a significant part of the history of Topeka, Kansas: *www.190arw.ang.af.mil/shared/media/document/AFD-090519-157.pdf.*

Air refueling has also played an important role in the history of military aviation: *www.amc.af.mil/news/story.asp?id=123144488.*

Chapter 14: Here Comes My Heart Now

White Lakes Mall, though ultimately not profitable for Fulmer and Meyers, was a significant project in the decade after the War. *www.mallsofamerica.blogspot.com/2006/04/white-lakes-mall.html.*

The McDonald's sign Royce talked about has a prominent place at the Kansas Museum of History. *www.kshs.org/p/museum-fast-food-exhibit/10666.*

No record of Topeka's "Pickle Man" exists.

Acknowledgements

Royce and I want to thank everyone who was so supportive of this project, especially Karon Fulmer. Her grammar skills and eye for detail are now legendary. If a mistake still exists, it belongs solely to us. Other watchful editing eyes were Colonel Pejakovich and Thea's son, Nathan Fredrickson. Because of Royce, Nate can now build a mean set of shelves. Thanks to the very creative Steve Fredrickson for the title. West Point graduate William H. Eggering, LTC (ret), U.S. Army, overwhelmed us with his generosity of time and friendship. With painstaking creativity and devotion to accuracy, Bill made a museum quality model of the B-24 D airplane with the Carpetbagger modifications.

Thea wants to thank her dear friend, Royce, for trusting her with his life story. I've loved spending time with you. I haven't laughed so much in years. But I am going to have to stop swearing like a damn Tech Sergeant.

Printed in Great Britain
by Amazon